Scott Cohen's Outdoor Kitchen Design Workbook

1st Edition

Copyright 2008 Intellectual Property Sales Inc.

All Rights Reserved.

(800) 813-8422

Special Thanks To:

HGTV

BCII

Participating Families

"The Host With The Most" Brandon Johnson

Authors: Scott Cohen and Elizabeth Lexau

Graphic Artist: Jose Hernandez

Illustrators: Jana Moungdang and Navin Kistan

Editors: Marie NyBlom and Elizabeth Lexau

The projects in this book were built by The Green Scene unless otherwise noted. To see more of our work go to www.GreenSceneLandscape.com

Let's Get Cooking!

Mmmm, barbecue! Hear it sizzle and pop; smell its enticing aroma; taste its smoky goodness. A backyard barbecue isn't just about food; it's a delectable experience for all the senses.

Some of my favorite childhood memories feature evenings around the barbecue with my family and our closest friends. I used to sit and admire my father's culinary skills. An expert at cooking the large roasts that were the highlight our family get-togethers, he was always the hero of the party. While the kids played chase and hide and seek, the grown-ups gathered around the grill to watch, wait, and toast the cook. Every so often an outburst of adult laughter would drown out our carefree shouts. Spirits were high and the night was always magic.

Many of us savor delicious memories like these. It's no wonder that our love of barbecue has transformed the outdoor cooking experience from the simple charcoal grill to something much more sophisticated: the outdoor kitchen.

In this book I offer homeowners, designers, and contractors some of my favorite ideas for creating outdoor kitchens that are beautiful and comfortable. Best of all, they really cook. I hope these ideas inspire you to create a backyard kitchen that lets you enjoy outdoor living as much as I do.

Copyright 2008 VerdantCustomOutdoors.com

Table of Contents

Outdoor Kitchens Are Hot!

As more homeowners create distinct outdoor rooms in their backyards, the outdoor kitchen has become the focal point. People have always congregated around food and drink. Outdoor kitchens take advantage of this tendency. Whether it's a night of revelry with a crowd, a relaxing evening with the family, or a romantic alfresco dinner for two, the outdoor kitchen serves as a natural gathering space that draws people together.

There's another reason outdoor kitchens are booming: property value. Homeowners recognize that an outdoor kitchen adds significant value to a home with a comparatively low investment. In some areas, outdoor kitchens have even become an expected amenity for a comfortable home. In others, an outdoor kitchen is a standout feature, offering a valuable edge in any housing market.

But practicality aside, outdoor kitchens are just plain fun. They're here to stay and the creative possibilities are endless.

Barbecue Beginnings

In the most traditional sense, barbeque refers to the method of slow-cooking meat at a low temperature with smoke. It most likely dates back to prehistoric times when a smoking process was used to preserve meats. Smoking was a preferred method over salting because the smoke also helped keep insects away from the meat.

The exact origin of the word "barbeque", however, remains controversial. Many believe the word comes from the Arawakan Indians of Hispaniola, who had a method of erecting a "barbacòa", a frame of wooden sticks over a fire for drying meat. Others hold that the word stems from a French saying, "barbe à queue", which translates into "beard to tail". This refers to the slow-cooking of a whole animal over a fire.

In the U.S., barbeque has a long history in the south. Barbeque was also especially popular with cowboys on western cattle drives. The cowboys would often be given poor, tough cuts of meat, which they tenderized by slow-cooking them over a fire. Little did these cowboys know their humble camp cookouts would live on long after their way of life had passed on.

DESIGN.
E. B. A. ZWOYER.
FUEL.
No. 27,483. Patented Aug. 3. 1897.

Fig: 1 Fig: 2 Fig: 3

Witnesses: Inventor.

The Original Charcoal Briquette

Ellsworth Zwoyer, of Reading, Pennsylvania, patented the first charcoal briquette in 1897 and began manufacturing them. In 1920, Henry Ford, an acquaintance of Zwoyer, got in the briquette game with the help of his friend Thomas Edison.

Ford actually used wood scraps, sawdust, and glue left over from his automobile assembly lines to create a clean, smoke-free source of heat. The keyword here is "smoke-free". While today many think of smoke as the secret to great barbeque, Ford was apparently only interested in heat production and not barbeque flavor.

E.G. Kingsford, a relative of Ford, eventually bought his invention and put the charcoal briquette into commercial production. While the initial purpose of the charcoal briquette was for heat in stoves and heaters, people soon be gan to use them for outdoor cooking. Today, we use the terms "barbecue", "barbeque", or simply "BBQ"to encompass most methods of outdoor cooking.

Be True To BBQ

BBQ = smoke + time
GRILLING = heat + fire

We often use the word barbeque, or simply BBQ, to refer to just about any kind of cookout today, but there's actually a difference between traditional barbecue and more common outdoor cooking methods. Barbecue refers to cooking food slowly with indirect heat and smoke. It usually involves large pieces of meat like pork roasts, beef brisket, and ribs. Wood-fired flames are typically used because they produce smoke, adding extra flavor that coals or propane lack.

Grilling, on the other hand, is a more direct, high-heat method of cooking. It uses a variety of heat sources including coals and gas-fired flames. Today, we also use the word BBQ to refer to any casual outdoor party involving grilled foods. Although the words and cooking methods vary, barbecue is a widely adopted social term for a custom that has become the highlight of summer get-togethers throughout North America.

Charcoal vs. Briquette

What's the difference?

Before the invention of the briquette, natural lump charcoal was king. For some outdoor cooks, it still is today. Charcoal is the product that results when wood is partially burned in a low oxygen environment. Water and other volatile components burn off leaving an irregularly shaped lump of carbon.

Briquettes are made of scrap wood and sawdust that are also partially burned into charcoal. But this charcoal is compressed with a starch binder and other additives and then molded into the briquette shape we all know. The uniform size, shape, and compression give charcoal briquettes a nice, even heat for grilling.

Charcoal briquettes are designed to burn slowly and consistently no matter what the air flow is in the grill. This is because the tight compression of the carbon makes it hard for oxygen to penetrate. When briquettes do burn, they also burn off the binding agents and other chemicals that hold them together.

Some cooks prefer to barbecue with natural lump charcoal. Lump charcoal burns very quickly when exposed to oxygen. It's best for cooks who want more control over the burn rate and temperature of the flames and who have a cooker that allows more precise adjustment of the flow of air to the flames.

Specialty Charcoals

There are a number of specialty charcoal variations on the market today. One of the most popular is embedded with wood chips such as mesquite or oak. These add smoke and flavor to the cooking fire. These work well, and there's no learning curve since they are used just like traditional briquettes.

Other specialty boutique charcoals are marketed as chemical-free or manufactured from certain types of wood. While more expensive, they offer purists an option from mass-produced charcoal.

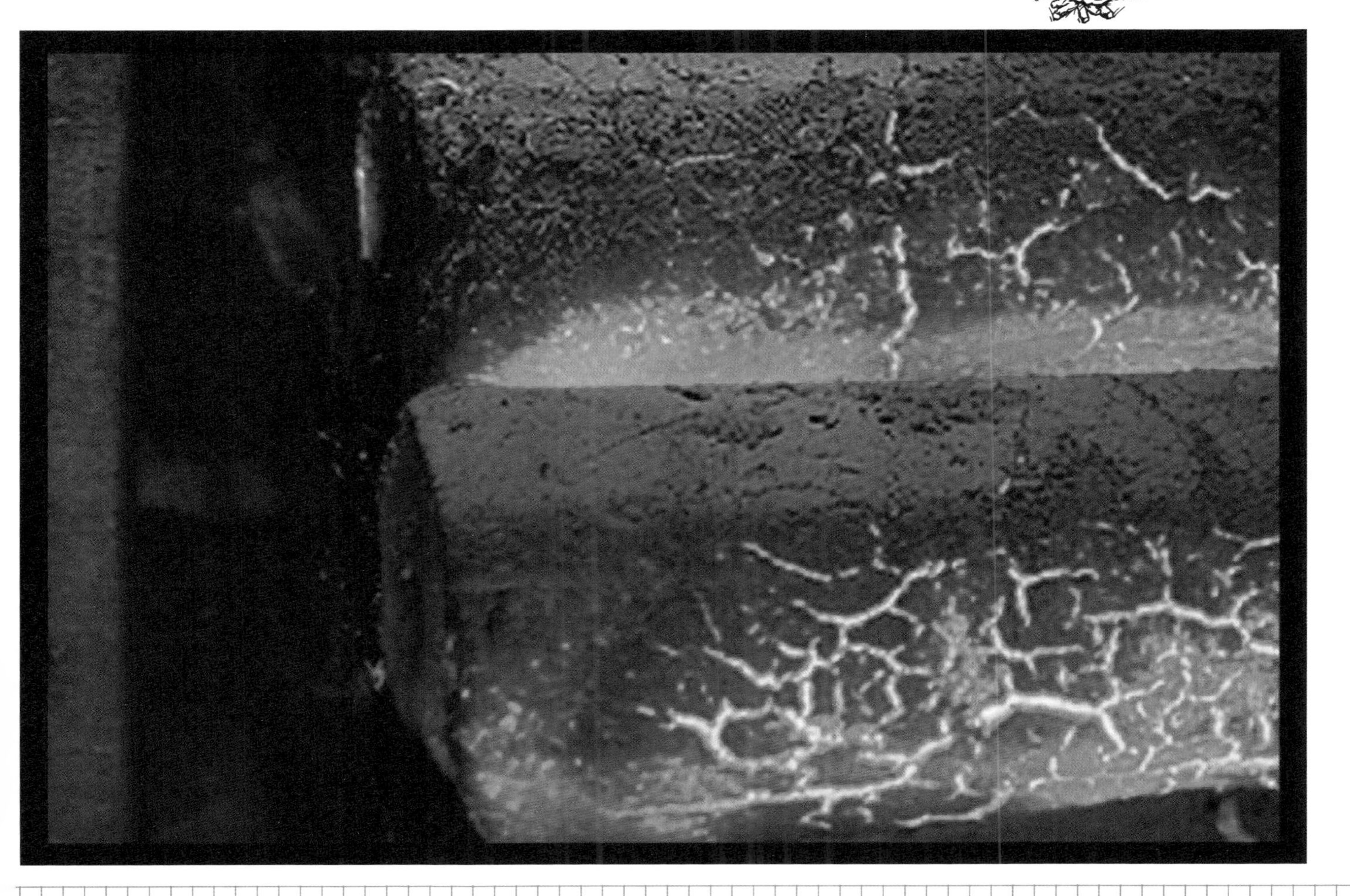

Do Your Homework

HGTV
Featuring Scott Cohen
Fetch-a-Sketch

Do Your Homework

Slaving over a hot stove has never been so enticing. With modern outdoor cooking spaces, today's homeowners are no longer fighting to get out of the kitchen; they're fighting to get into it.

If you're designing a new outdoor kitchen, it's important to do some homework first. I know, I know, homework never sounds like fun. But great spaces take thoughtful planning, and planning takes time. Doing some thinking now will save you from regret later. No one wants to finish up a project thinking "I wish I'd done this" or "I shoulda thoughta that."

So Many Options

No two backyard cooks are alike. A well-designed kitchen should meet the unique cooking, entertaining, and dining needs of the homeowner. It must be sized to meet the space available and should be located to take full advantage of the property's assets. Most of all, it should be equipped to make cooking outdoors as fun for the chef as it is for the guests.

The possibilities are endless and sometimes overwhelming. To help define the parameters of your design, start with the list of questions on the following pages. As you continue planning, keep checking back and adapting this list.

These preliminary questions will get you started as you identify your own personal style.

This contemporary cast concrete counter was hand seeded with blue, white and clear glass chips. The glass blocks are enhanced by fiber-optic lighting cables that weave back and forth between each course of block.

Mosaic tiles bridge the gap between the dual level countertops. Lights added in this riser help illuminate the counter space for nighttime entertaining.

The raised backsplash on this counter helps screen the close-by neighbors. Raised bar height counter provides a place for friends to hang out with the chef!

Find Your Style

- 1. Do you have a style or theme in mind for your new space?

- 2. What styles catch your eye when you flip through magazines or visit the homes of others?

- 3. How would you describe the architectural style of your home? What are its key features?

- 4. What are your hobbies, your most memorable vacations, your favorite destinations? Can you incorporate these into your style or design?

Photo by Deidra Walpole - Custom Mosaic Backsplash Tile By MichelleGriffoul.com

Entertaining Needs

- 1. How often do you cook outside?
- 2. How many people do you entertain outdoors on a regular basis? How many people might you have at your biggest party?
- 3. Will you need to accommodate a bartender and/or a caterer?
- 4. If you'll have a dining table, how many people would you like to seat?
- 5. What kind of furniture do you see in your new space?
- 6. How much space would the furniture require?

Counter Configuration

- 1. How much food preparation space will you need in a counter?
- 2. Do you want the counter built at one height or would you like a split level counter with a portion devoted to food preparation and a portion at bar height? (Industry standards call for cooking counters at 36"and bar counters at 42".)
- 3. If you opt for a bar counter, how many people would you like to accommodate there?

Equipment Wish List

1. How large a grill do you plan to use?

2. What basic appliances and accessories do you want to include in your layout? (See page 102 for ideas)

3. What are your "must-haves"? What are your "it-would-be-nice-to-haves"?

Lighting & Fire

1. Will you be doing a lot of cooking and entertaining after dark? What parts of your space are most important to light?

2. Will you be eating outdoors on cool nights? Would a fireplace or another heat source make you and your guests more comfortable?

Kitchen Placement

1. Is there an area in the yard that you think would perform best for the outdoor kitchen?

2. How do your outdoor spaces and indoor spaces relate to each other? Where are the doors to the house? How will you bring food and other items from the indoor kitchen to the outdoor one and back?

3. Will some of your parties be indoor/outdoor? Where will the outdoor kitchen best enhance this option?

4. What is the prevailing wind direction?

5. What are the sun and shade angles in the yard?

6. Does your yard have a view? Who would you like to most enjoy the view? Guests? Cook? Both?

7. What are your needs for privacy?

Location, Location,

Location

The Golden Rule Of Design

"Form Follows Function" - You've no doubt heard this elementary design principle before. It's helpful to embrace it throughout every step of your planning. Whenever you're faced with decisions regarding your outdoor kitchen, think about how it will best function for your cooking, dining, and entertaining needs. Then design a beautiful form around that function. Consider function now as you choose your location.

What's the best place in the yard to put your new outdoor kitchen? This question deserves careful consideration because the answer can have a huge impact in how often you use your new space, how convenient it is, and how much you and your guests enjoy being there.

Keep It Close

For starters, think of your new outdoor room as an extension of your home, not necessarily a separate destination. Keeping it close to the house is usually a good idea. This will make your outdoor kitchen more convenient for food preparation and outdoor entertaining. It will also make it much more fun for the cook.

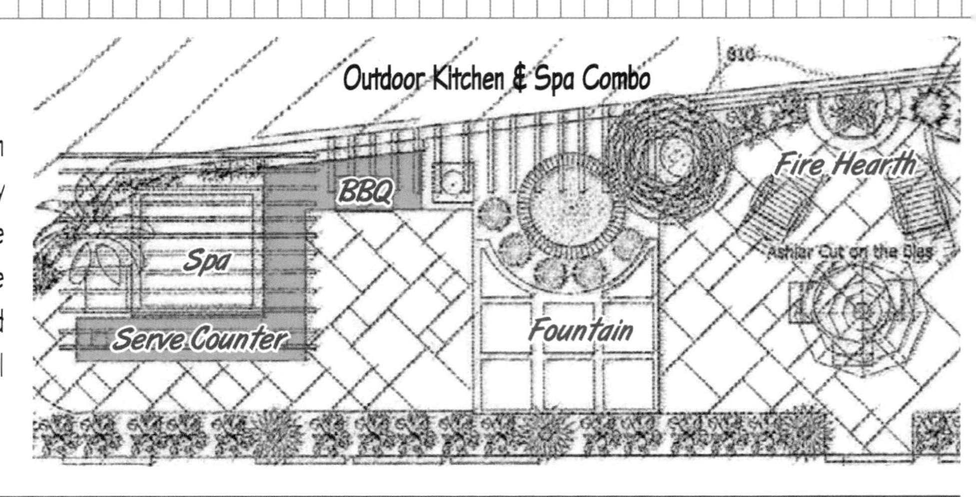

This small backyard exemplifies good outdoor room design, providing separate spaces for cooking, entertaining, and dining. A well-placed fountain helps cool the space and give the backyard a courtyard resort-like feel.

Keep It Convenient

Some people think they should locate their kitchen in a distant under-used part of their property. Using the logic, "if-we-build-it-they-will-come," they think a distant kitchen will serve as a focal point that will draw guests away from the house further into the yard.

But this logic can backfire. For one thing, most food prep usually takes place in the indoor kitchen. A long hike from the BBQ to the indoor kitchen can get old very quickly. Remember, grilling requires monitoring. If you run out of BBQ sauce or need more beer, you want to be able to grab it from the kitchen quickly without risking scorched food. In the worst case scenario, that long walk might keep you from using your new outdoor kitchen as much as you could. We can't have that.

Keep 'Em Together

Keeping your guests together and keeping your outdoor cook happy is another reason for locating the outdoor kitchen nearby. No matter how comfortable the outdoor space, some people will always congregate in or near the house – either because they're chatting with the indoor cook, checking the score of the game on TV, or greeting new arrivals.

This can break up a great party or leave a lonely cook who keeps missing the punch line when it's time to check the food. If the grill is close to the house, the cook can dash in, grab a cocktail, tell a joke, and be back on duty with no danger of medium-rare turning into well-done.

Kiss The Cook

Please keep an eye on my dinner..

Notice how people are always congregating around the cook? Think they're there to keep you company? Think again. Nine times out of ten, they're checking up on you to make sure you don't wreck their dinner.

If you do need to locate the kitchen further from the house, it's not a disaster. Just make sure it truly is "the" place to be. Add plenty of fun elements there to keep the party together. Include extra storage and food prep space to cut down on trips to the house. And make sure your beverage center is always well-stocked.

Keep It Beautiful

Pay attention to the views of and from your proposed outdoor kitchen from all angles. It helps to start with a plot drawing of your house and yard. Snap sight lines from windows and doors in the house toward the yard. Do the same from various spots in the outdoor space. Be aware of the best views (and any eyesores), and design around them.

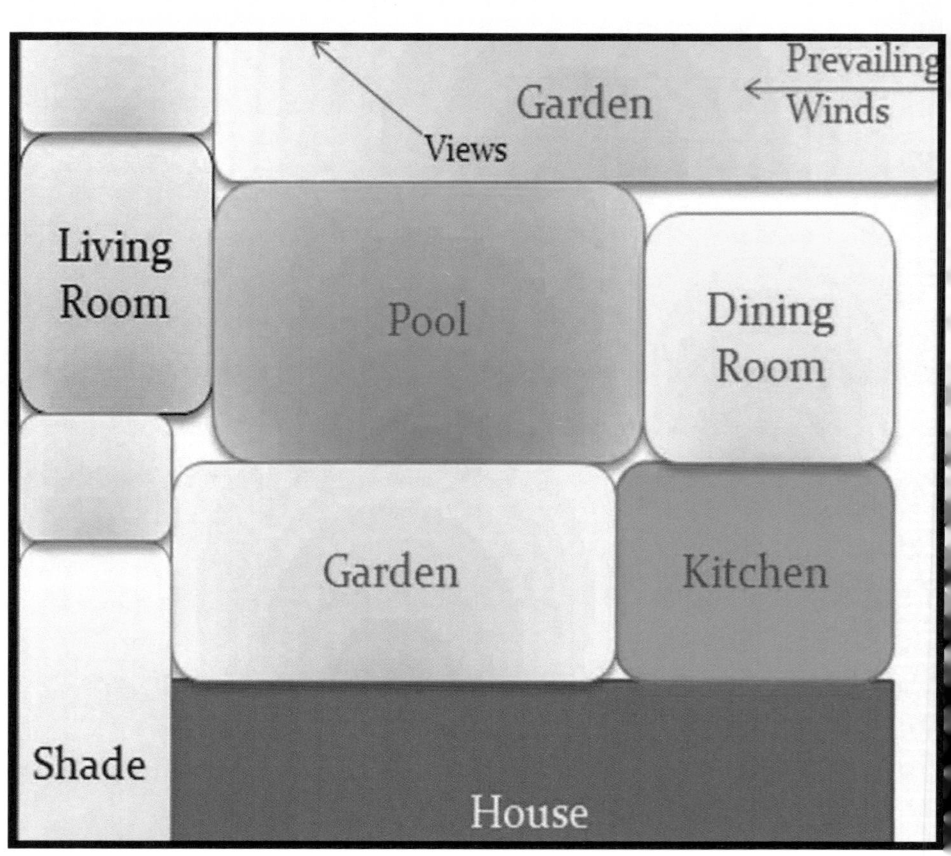

Create a Bubble Plan

Create an initial bubble plan to help visualize the influential design parameters (wind, sun, shade, traffic flow, views, etc.). Draw freeflowing shapes to define these outdoor rooms. More specific measurements can be defined later in the design process.

The View From The Inside

How will your outdoor kitchen impact views from the house? Look at the sight lines you've drawn from windows and doors that face the yard. Make sure the placement of counters and other elements will enhance your existing views – not detract from them.

Does your kitchen or dining room window currently look out on a gorgeous seascape or at your treasured rose garden? If so, don't destroy that beautiful picture. Instead, design around it. If possible, keep the new room out of that sight line. If elements of the kitchen need to be placed within that view, keep them low and beautiful, so they frame the picture instead of distracting from it.

This doesn't mean you should hide your outdoor kitchen from indoor viewing. Just the opposite, your new space should be so striking you'll want to look at it from indoors and out. Try to position the most attractive features so they can be seen from the house; place the more utilitarian components accordingly. When you're standing at your French door, would you rather see a decorative element, like a gorgeous tile mosaic or wrought iron art piece, or a stainless steel grill hood? (Of course, if it's the stainless that turns you on, that's o.k. too).

The location of this stunning covered outdoor kitchen frames the magnificent views beyond. The placement of columns and equipment leaves ample counter space.

This cast concrete counter was poured in Davis brand "Adobe" integral colored concrete and was wet sanded after the initial cure. The counter veneer is authentic stacked stone in 1"-3" pre-cut panels.

The kitchen features a 54" Viking grill, dual side burner, storage pantry doors, fridge and multiple electrical outlets. A stainless steel warming drawer keeps your buns warm and ready!

What About The Cook?

Don't forget the cook when considering the views, but avoid focusing too much on the view from the grill. While you may imagine yourself gazing at distant mountains while turning the shish kabobs, the reality is that when you're cooking, you're usually looking at the food (at least you should be). When you lift the hood of the grill to check the roast, you'll be blocking your view anyway.

If you have to make a choice between the cook and the guest for prime real estate, treat your guests to the view. Pay attention to your cooking and reward yourself later when you join your company.

Top 10 Plants For Outdoor Screening

1. Fern Pine (Podocarpus gracilior) - Not in the pine family at all, Podocarpus is an evergreen tree grown in a columnar form. Leaf drop is light is inconspicuous.

2. Ficus microcarpa nitida 'Green Gem' - Deep green waxy leaves and dense growing habit make this an ideal tree for screening. Planted in columnar form this tree can reach 20' or be easily maintained at a shorter height with bi-monthly pruning. Use root barriers when planting ficus close to walls or structures.

3. Carolina Cherry (Prunus caroliniana) - Great in coastal areas, this tree can be puned as a 20' hedge and reaches 40' when allowed to grow untrimmed.

4. Wax Leaf Privet (Ligustrum texanum) - This evergreen shrub can be a 10' high narrow hedge. Privet responds well to pruning and can take any shape you choose. This plant is used often to create artistic topiary.

5. Sweet Olive (Osmanthus fragrans) - This shrub has similar growth habits to the Wax Leaf Privet although the foliage is not quite as dense and requires a little more training to keep a tight hedge. This shrub is very fragrant with tiny inconspicuous white flowers that smell terrific! Think "freesia" or "apricot blossoms".

6. Eugenia - Watch for psyllids and treat early with system insect control, deep watering and regular fertilization.

7. Viburnum japonicum - 10-20' tall with large glossy leaves.

8. Italian Cypress (Cupressus sempervirens) Narrow columnar to 60.'

9. Purple Hopseed Bush (Dodonea viscosa 'Purporea') 6-15' tall.

10. Photinia fraserii - Shurb or small tree to 10-15' tall.

Photos courtesy of BambooPipeline.com

Screening And Privacy

Consider privacy when choosing a site for your new space. Most people don't want to be in plain sight of their neighbors when entertaining or relaxing with the family. You can choose a site with existing privacy or create a more secluded space with the addition of structures or natural elements like shrubs, hedges, and trees.

You can use elements like these to screen unattractive views or eyesores too. If screening will require a permanent structure, make sure to check local building codes, setbacks, or home-owners association guidelines before deciding on a site for your outdoor room.

Special Section: "Get Out, Way Out!" Double Outdoor Kitchens

Fire and water make a great combination. This project shown here and on the following pages was showcased on the HGTV show "Get Out, Way Out!" It featured two outdoor kitchens: one close to the house and the second swim-up kitchen is under the pavilion.

Photo by Paul C. Jonason
HGTV
Featuring Scott Cohen

Photo by Paul C. Jonason

Photo by Paul C. Jonason

Mind The Elements

Wind and sun can greatly impact your comfort in the outdoors. Consider both when you choose a building site for your outdoor kitchen.

Location Check List

- Views
- Wind
- Proximity
- Utilities
- Privacy

Hot Tip: Whenever possible, avoid placing dining patios downwind of smoke.

Sun and Shade

Outdoor cooking often takes place in the heat of the day during summer months. Locate your outdoor kitchen under existing shade or plan to add new sources of shade. Natural shade from trees and vines is best. In addition to providing well-ventilated shelter from harsh sunlight, plants provide a natural cooling effect as they release moisture into the air through transpiration. Deciduous plantings lose their leaves in winter, allowing the sun to shine in when it's more welcome.

You may need to add a structure, such as a trellis or pergola, to provide shade in places where it doesn't already exist. When designing shade bars on your structure, consider sun angles. Again, when creating any permanent structure, remember to check local building codes.

ShadeTree awning

Watch The Wind

Pay attention to the direction of prevailing winds and to where winds will take any smoke from your outdoor kitchen. New smoker drawers add wonderful flavor but if you use them, you're going to generate a lot of smoke over a number of hours. Give that smoke somewhere to go where it won't bother people.

Consider the proximity of the outdoor kitchen to doors, windows, and balconies on the house. Position the BBQ or smoking drawers so that smoke has space to dissipate before hitting these. Finally, be a good neighbor. Try to locate the grill where it won't blow too much smoke into the next yard. (If you can't, make sure to invite your neighbors over for BBQ on a regular basis.)

Hot Tips for Cool Shade:
Use built-in umbrella stands to add flexible shading options throughout the yard, especially over BBQ counters. These inexpensive pre-cast PVC units work well for standard size umbrellas (though they don't fit oversize umbrellas). They are often sold as volleyball net stands and can be purchased through any swimming pool supplier.

Retractable awning and shade canopies like these offered by ShadeTree (as shown on page 34), are another inexpensive option for creating shade over the outdoor kitchen area. These custom made awnings cover large, small, and irregularly shaped areas. They're available in dozens of weather-resistant fabrics to coordinate with your outdoor furniture.

What About Power?

Access to gas and electric lines is another consideration when it comes to locating your outdoor kitchen. Although utility access can be changed to some degree, it isn't always cost-effective to make major changes. Sometimes limitations exist that aren't apparent to the average homeowner. Early in the design process, you'll want to consult with an electrician to evaluate your needs and look for any access issues that may be present on your site.

Don't assume that one outlet in the back of the house is going to be adequate to provide the juice you need to power up your new outdoor kitchen. Most kitchens require their own breaker with enough electricity to power a rotisserie, blender, hot plate or warming drawer, refrigerator, and lighting. Many of these, especially refrigerators and warming drawers, have significant power requirements.

The size and layout of the kitchen will also dictate your site choice. Your new space may call for a footprint that makes it best suited for a particular place in your yard. So before you go further, turn to the next chapter to size up your new space.

Photos on this page by Deidra Walpole

Sizing & Layout

While you're thinking about the ideal location for your outdoor kitchen, you also need to consider size and layout. What appliances do you want in your new kitchen and how much space will you need to accommodate them? What's the best way to position counters, seating areas, and cooking zones?

Size, placement, and layout decisions need to be made together. You may have the perfect spot in mind for your new outdoor room, but when you start adding up the space you'll need, you might discover that the kitchen you envision won't quite fit there.

Don't panic. With careful planning and fresh ideas, you can determine the space you need, maximize the space you have, and create an arrangement that works perfectly in your garden.

Scale

Lets start with the big picture first. What's the ideal size for an outdoor kitchen? The bigger the better, right? Not exactly. Even if your yard will accommodate a huge, expansive, blow-your-mind BBQ, it may not look so great next to your house. Remember, your outdoor room is an extension of your home. It should compliment your house, not compete with it. The size of your outdoor kitchen should reflect the amount of time you realistically plan to use it. If your family enjoys grilling out whenever you can – for everyday meals as well as parties – your kitchen should be big enough to make it convenient to use every day. On the other hand, if you realistically see yourself using the BBQ only occasionally, scale back the cooking area. Save the rest of your yard for other features...fireplace, spa, gazebo, pond, waterfall, fountain, I could go on...

This small backyard was a challenge for our HGTV "Get Out, Way Out!" episode. The client wanted a swim-up bar off the spa, outdoor kitchen, fire pit, seat walls and plenty of patio space, all in a very tight area. The smaller the yard, the more attention you need to pay to the ergonomics (science related to the amount of space a human body needs to do his work).

The Golden Rule...Again

Remember the rule of design that we brought up in the previous chapter? Form Follows Function. To determine the best size for your space, first decide what outdoor kitchen components you need to accommodate, then design around them.

Most outdoor kitchens need space for several distinct functions. These might include prepping food, cooking it, serving it, dining, and hanging out. Don't think that these spaces all have to fit together on one big slab of patio. In some gardens, the cooking, dining, and mingling all take place in a relatively compact space with the aid of some well-placed and well-proportioned bar/dining counters. In others, things are broken up a bit to create a series of small rooms that flow together beautifully and comfortably.

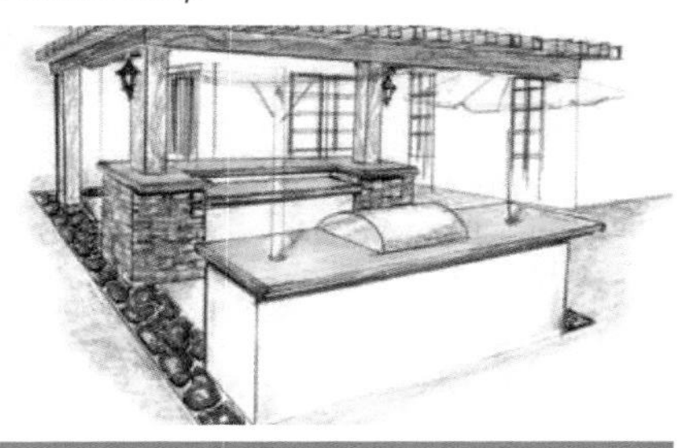

Do You Really Need It?
Think about your regular entertaining needs before choosing accessories. What about that beer tap Kegerator? It sure sounds like fun, but be ready to drink a lot of beer. Kegs only stay fresh for three to four weeks. It's a must-have if you frequently hold big sports parties or always have plenty of beer-drinking friends on hand. If not, save the money and space for something you'll really use.

Photo by Patrick Stringer

This kitchen was our first opportunity to try the new rubber rope edge. The spectacular results emphasized the endless benefits of cast concrete countertops!

Get In The Zone

For indoor kitchens, designers often talk about the working triangle. But with outdoor kitchens, it's often better to think in terms of zones:
Prep Zone, Cooking Zone, Serving Zone and Entertaining Zone.

To figure out how much room you need for prepping and cooking, start with an outline of the features you want. Use the list of appliances and accessories on page 102, starting with the grill itself. Be inclusive, but don't go overboard. Some of these kitchen accessories sound like so much fun, you may feel like you just gotta have 'em. But if you're going to spend the money or dedicate space for another fun gadget, you want to make sure you'll really use it.

Take the grill for example. If you see yourself simmering a large vat of beans or boiling corn on the cob as you BBQ your baby back ribs, you'll probably find side burners really helpful. But think it through. Envision your actual cooking style and entertainment needs. Maybe additional grilling space will come in handier for your parties than a side burner or two.

Remember to keep scale in mind here too. Will all of your accessories require an outdoor kitchen that dwarfs the rest of your backyard? Will enlarging your cooking space shrink your dining and hangout space? There's really no point in installing a 54-inch grill if you can only entertain 15 people at a time.

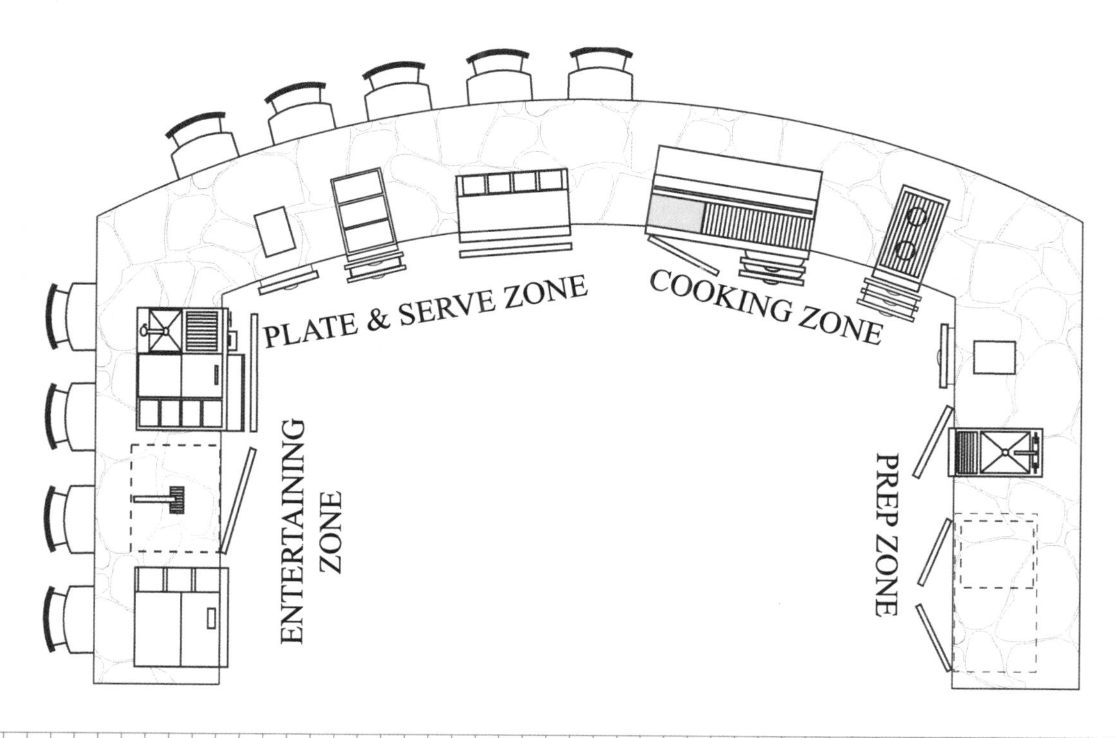

Graphic complements of AlfrescoGrills.com

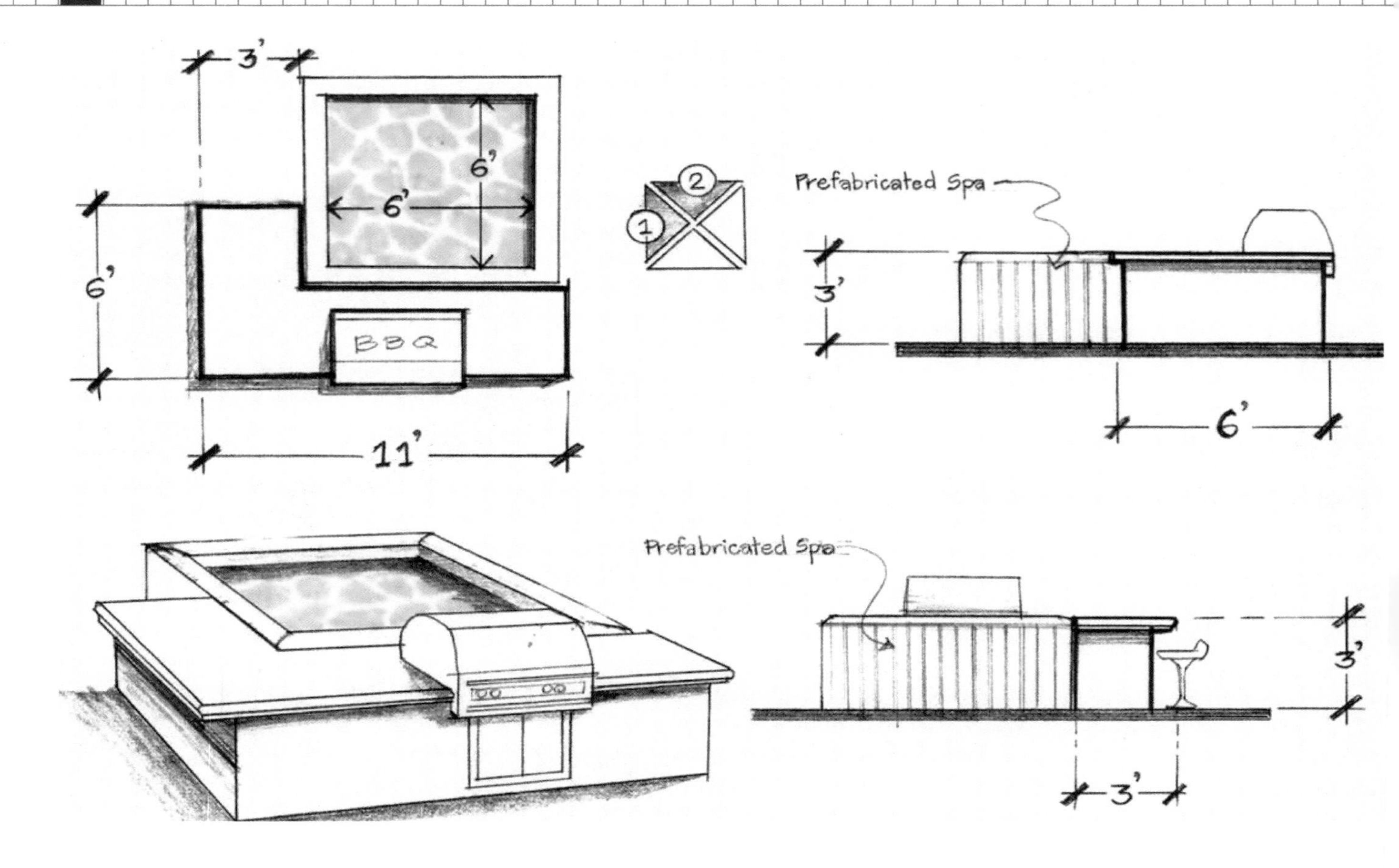

Counter Measures

The cooking area doesn't only include appliances, of course. It should also include counter space, and plenty of it. Counters play a major role in the basic layout of your kitchen. They also play a huge role in setting the style and tone of the space. See Eye Appeal: Counters, Flooring, and More for more on counter style.

Various counters might be dedicated to prepping food, serving it, relaxing at the bar, and dining. It's important to know how much space you'll want for each of these activities.

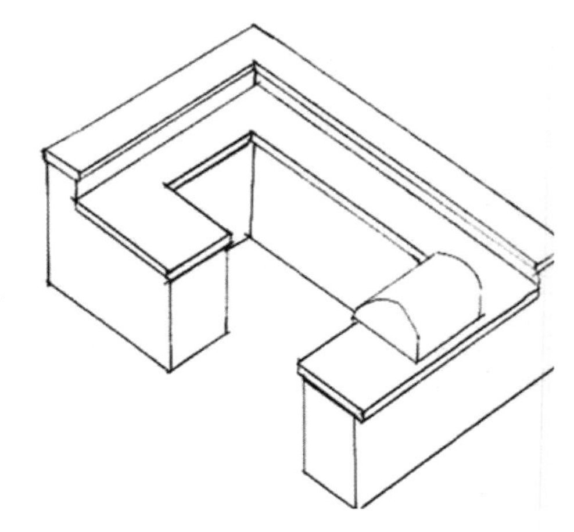

In many kitchens, counters will serve more than one function. For example a serve counter may hold a buffet or be used as a dining or beverage bar. It's important for counters to be sized appropriately for all of their jobs.

In the food prep area, allow counter surface for any cutting, skewering, and other food handling that will be done outdoors. It's also very important to leave at least 12 to 14 inches of counter space between appliances or accessories to accommodate a serving platter. This way you'll have a spot to set your salmon steaks before you grill them and a place to put your steaming corn when you take it out of the kettle.

Serve Counters

To size up serve counters, decide if you'll do all your serving in one area or whether it might be better do divide functions into different serve stations – for example, a buffet for food and a separate beverage center for drinks.

For food serving stations, count the actual number of dishes you typically offer and - budget space for all of them. Allow room for condiments, plates, cups, and cutlery. Will you serve beverages here too? If so allow extra space for pre-poured or self-serve drinks.

Watch Traffic

Make sure there's good traffic flow around any serve counter by avoiding a dead-end at the bottom of the buffet. In many outdoor kitchens, the food buffet does double duty as the bar. To prevent traffic jams, provide an easy and obvious exit strategy for everyone using that serve station. Think grocery store checkout: pick up your dinner and move on through.

Storage

You'll want cupboards and drawers to keep your BBQ "tools of the trade" handy. You don't want to run to the house to get basic items for every outdoor meal. Plan to equip your kitchen with its own set of knives, bowls, towels, napkins, oven mitts, a corkscrew, and other items you'll use at every cookout. Then design your storage areas around these items.

Storage units are generally made from stainless steel. As with indoor kitchens you can choose different sizes and configurations that fit the items you'll be storing.

Clean Up

Don't forget the garbage. Nothing will sully the face of your beautiful new outdoor kitchen more than a large garbage bag or big gray plastic bin propped up against the counter. Plan under-counter space for the trash and recycling you'll generate during your evenings outdoors. Drop-through trash bins work great and are easy and economical to include in your design.

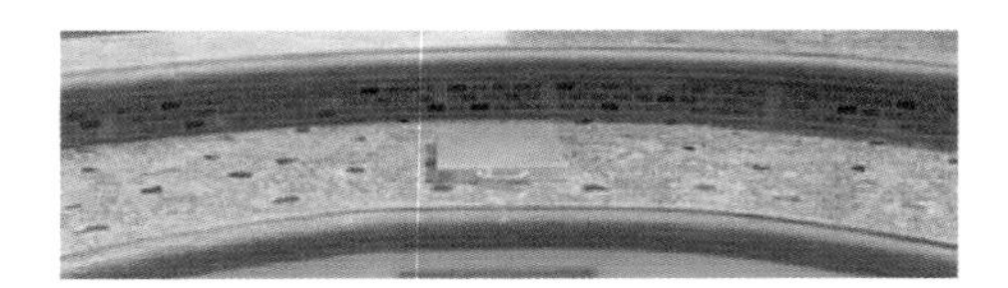

How Much Grill?

Remember, do the math: it's no use having a grill that can cook 40 burgers at a time if your backyard can only hold 15 people comfortably.

Typically a 32" to 42" grill is generous enough to serve your family and most get-togethers. Consider upsizing to closer to 50" if you regularly cook for large crowds.

Another option to consider is two smaller grills. Often the cost of two small grills is about the same as one giant one. With this setup you don't need to worry about the weight of the hood and you may even find two to be more convenient and versatile than one. On family nights, you might fire up only one grill. For bigger events, you can rotisserie the chicken on one BBQ and sear the veggies on another. You can also set up the second grill for smoking or use it as a warmer. Some people opt to use charcoal in their second grill to have the best of both worlds.

Do the Math

- Here are some industry standards to keep in mind as you're planning your counters:
- Standard food prep counters are 36" high. Sometimes it's necessary to raise the height to 38" to accommodate a fridge. A comfortable range for most is 36" to 38". Never exceed the height of the cook's bent elbow or you'll have a grumpy chef with sore shoulders.
- Bar serve counters vary from 42" to 46" high. Bar stools are typically 28" but this can vary greatly depending on styling and manufacturer. If your plan calls for bar stools, choose these first. Then let the seat height dictate final bar counter height.
- Bar counters should be at least 18" deep. This leaves ample room to accommodate most plates, which vary in diameter from about 9" to 11".
- Allow 24" width for each seat at the bar.
- The standard height for tabletops is 30".

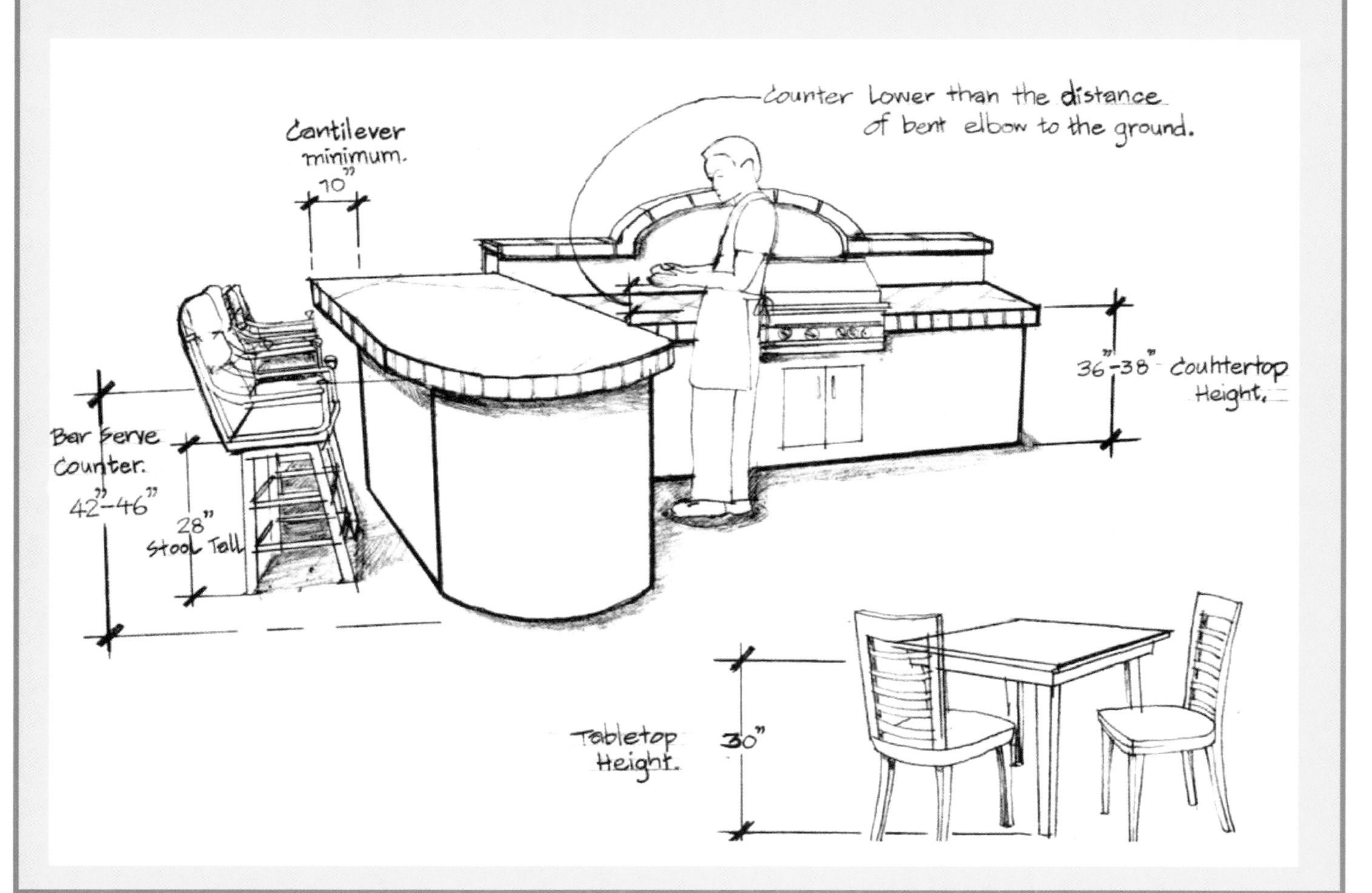

This outdoor kitchen was my first tri-level cast-concrete counter, with levels set at table height (30"), counter height (36" to 38") and bar-height (42" to 44"). The counter was cast with small coral pebbles and recycled amber glass in Davis brand "Sandstone" integral color.

HGTV
Featuring Scott Cohen

8 Fabulous Layouts

Basic Stand Alone Counter

Here are eight basic BBQ layouts that work for many different gardens sizes, but by no means are these all of the shapes you can create. Use these and other photos in this book to get a good idea of what shape is best for your outdoor kitchen.

- Basic stand alone counter
- Built-in table
- L - shaped return
- U-shape
- Split levels for bar service
- Basic with serve island
- 3/4 square
- Separate cook, prep, and serve sections

Find more layout ideas at
Fetch-A-Sketch.com
or OutdoorKitchenDesignIdeas.com

Built In Table

L-Shape Bar Height Return

L-Shape Return

U-Shape

U-Shape

Split Levels for Bar Service

Split Levels for Bar Service

Basic With Serve Island

Basic With Serve Island

3/4 Square

3/4 Square

Separate Cook Prep
& Serve Sections

Separate Cook Prep
& Serve Sections

Brandon Johnson, host of HGTV's "Get Out, Way Out!" is once again entertaining the ladies.

Fetch-a-Sketch.com

Clink, Clink Mingle, Mingle

Remember, in outdoor kitchens, the chopping, basting, and flipping often takes place in close proximity to the mingling, flirting, and glass-clinking. To keep everyone in the right zone, it's important to choose a layout that not only works well for cooking but also makes for a fun, comfortable party. The grill itself is often the center attraction. Make sure there's plenty of space nearby for several people to sit and watch the action. "Nearby" doesn't mean "next to". Your guests shouldn't feel like they're risking singed eyebrows when their supervising the cook.

In addition to spaces at a bar or dining counter, many backyard kitchens include additional areas for dining and relaxing. Again, don't think you need a space big enough to accommodate all your guests in one large expanse. Instead, the zone approach works best here too. Think about human party behavior and observe it at the next get together you attend. Instead of gathering in one big 'herd', people at a larger party will naturally group together in small conversational clusters. Design your dining and mingling areas around this tendency by providing several "outdoor rooms" to accommodate small groups. A series of interconnected spaces is a better fit for many yards and also creates a more inviting atmosphere. Provide destinations in the garden by connecting these gathering spots with welcoming pathways (this is called 'wayfinding' in the designer biz). Use focal points, seat walls, fountains, ponds, arbors, and fragrant plantings to create interest at different locations and draw guests out into the yard space.

HGTV
Featuring Scott Cohen

Types Of Outdoor Rooms

HGTV
Featuring Scott Cohen

This project was featured on HGTV's "Sizzling Outdoor Kitchens" as one of the greatest design spaces in the country to "grill and chill"!

There are many types of rooms you can add in conjunction with your outdoor kitchen. Use the design guide in the back of this book to create your own layouts.

Outdoor Dining Room

Size this patio based on the number of people you plan to host regularly. A 48" round table can seat 6-8 people depending on the size of the chairs. The minimum patio diameter that will accommodate one 48" round table is 10' 6". This allows enough space to pull out chairs, but not much walk-around space. For larger patios designed to accommodate more than one table, leave a three foot buffer zone to accommodate passing guests. A minimum 12' to 14' diameter allotment for each 48" round table will provide this buffer.

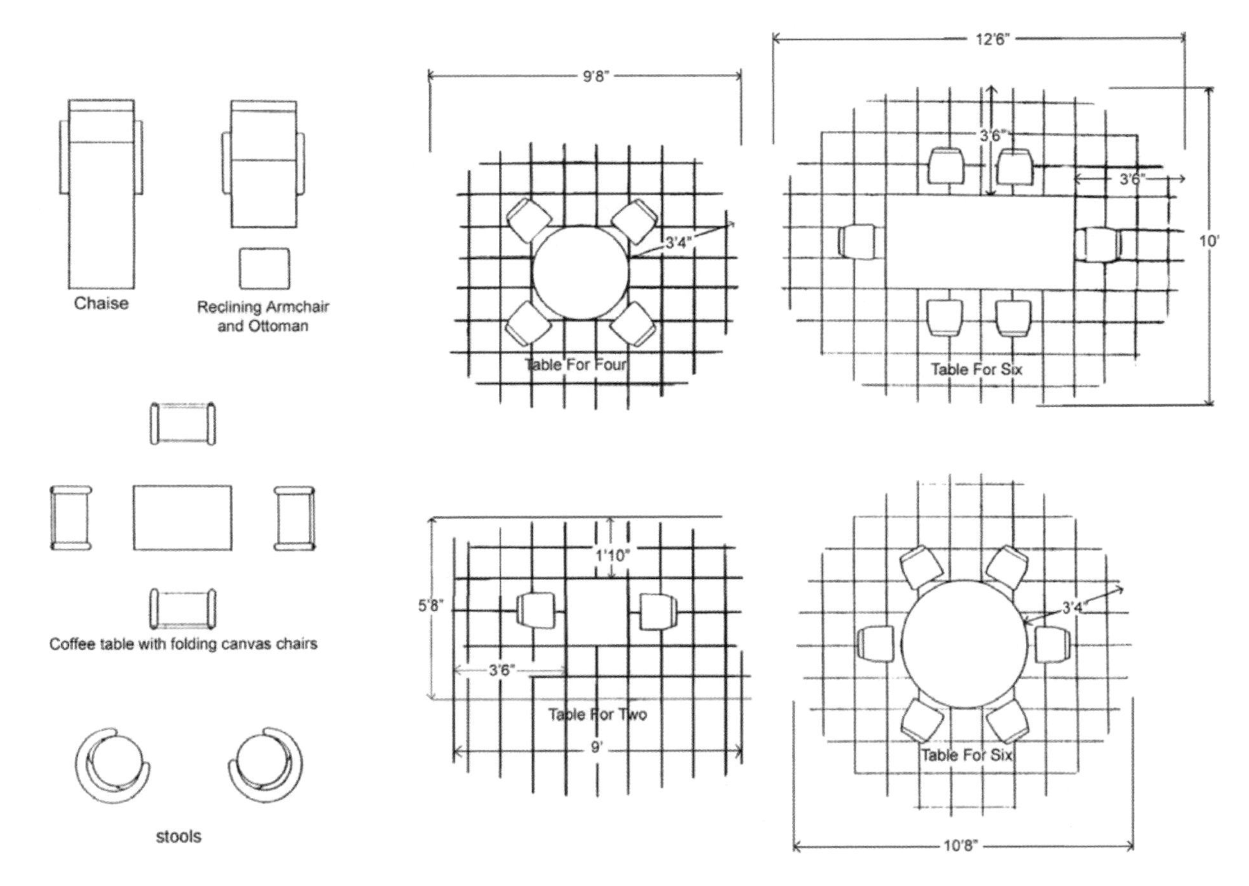

Outdoor Living Room

A Living Room Patio - Size this patio around the furniture you'll use here. A big trend in outdoor living room furniture is using "deep seating" patio furniture. Deep seating mimics your indoor couch, love seats, lounge chairs and coffee table styling. A good rule of thumb is to size living room areas at approximately 16' by 18'. Where possible, leave a 3' pathway clear of furniture to allow for good traffic flow through the garden.

The proximity of this outdoor kitchen, set close to the house and pool, keeps it close to the action and convenient for frequent trips indoors. The overall design epitomizes "outdoor room design" and was featured on HGTV/NBC's documentary on the latest trends in outdoor space design titled "Property Buzz"

Bistro Patio

Many homeowners and their guests appreciate a small, more intimate space to enjoy a meal for two or a quiet conversation. A small patio that accommodates a two-seater bistro table works well here and can be created almost anywhere including a side yard or in little back corner destination spots. A good standard size for a patio area like this is about 6' to 7' in diameter.

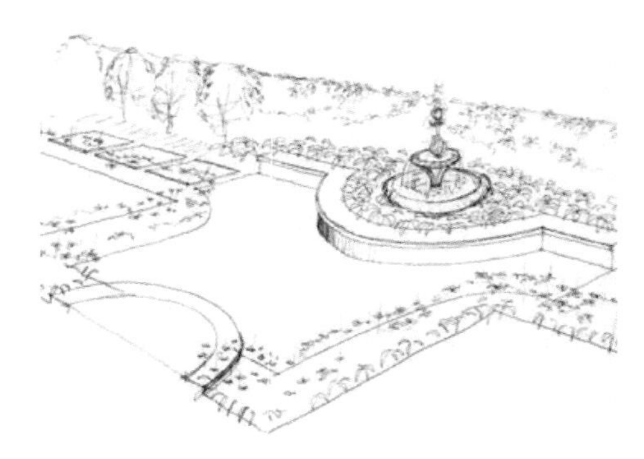

Keep It Green

Use grass and ground covers to break up pathways between patios. Place flower beds between structures, such as the house or walls, and patio areas. Even narrow 2' wide planting beds will soften edges and give the yard a more inviting, garden-like feel.

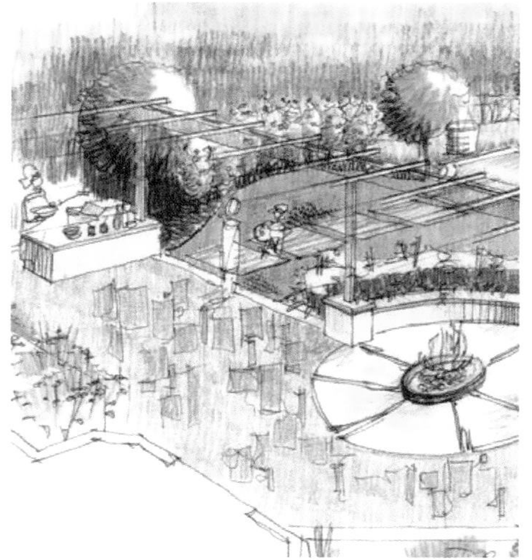

Start Creating

Use the templates in the back of this book to experiment with different layouts that will work in your yard. Photocopy the pages (you'll probably want several copies). Then cut out the pieces you need and arrange them in a few configurations that fit your space.

The furniture layouts are set to scale (1/4" equals 1 foot) so every inch counts.
Whenever you make permanent improvements to your property, it's important to consult a designer or contractor before coming up with a final design/layout.

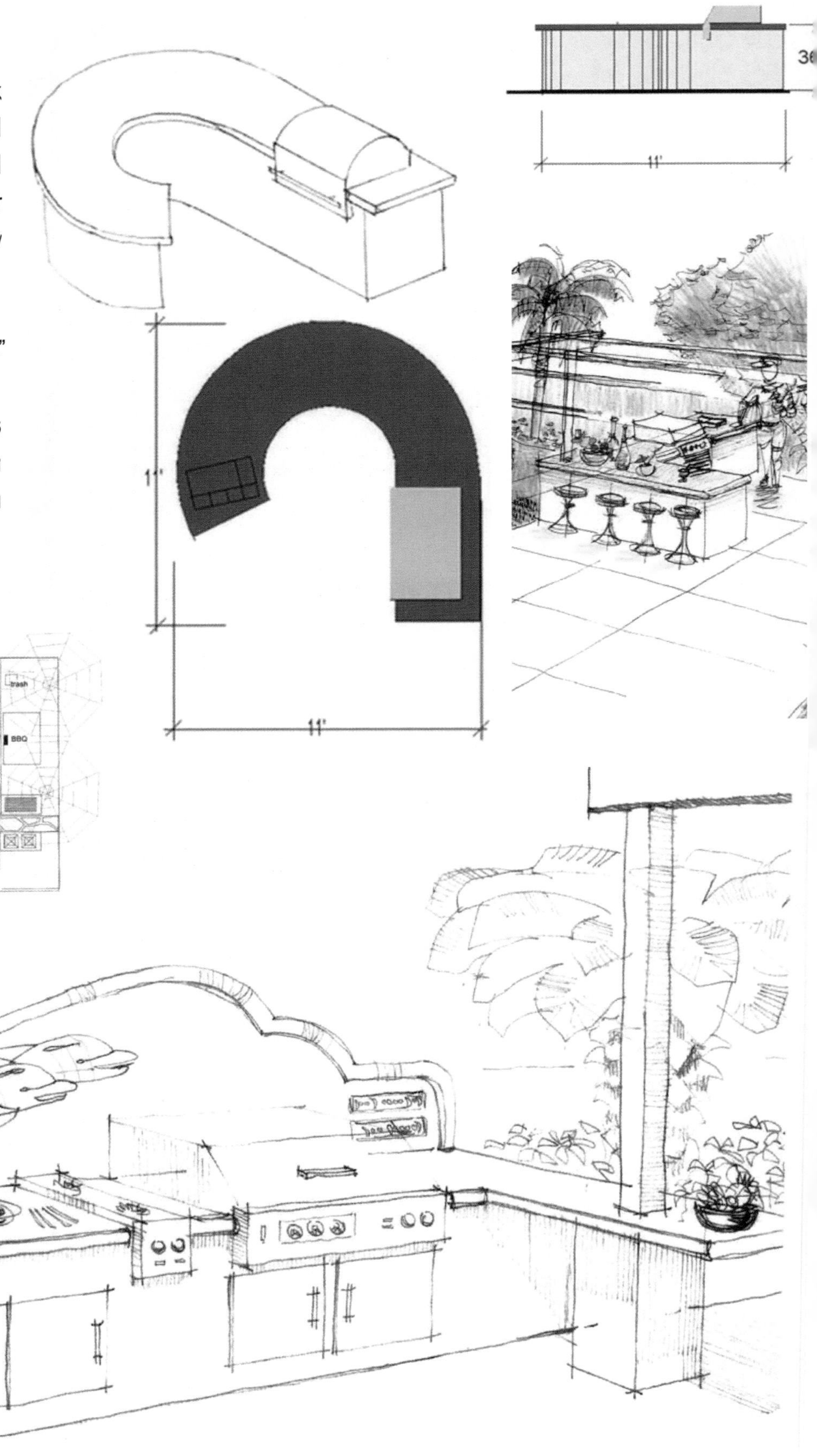

Patio Sizing Tip:
Landscape and patio furniture sizing kits are available from The Board Space Planning System (SpacePlanning.com). These easy-to-use magnetic boards will help you visualize your space to ensure adequate patio sizing. Flip them over and photocopy to capture multiple design options. These are dynamite planning tools for homeowners and professionals.

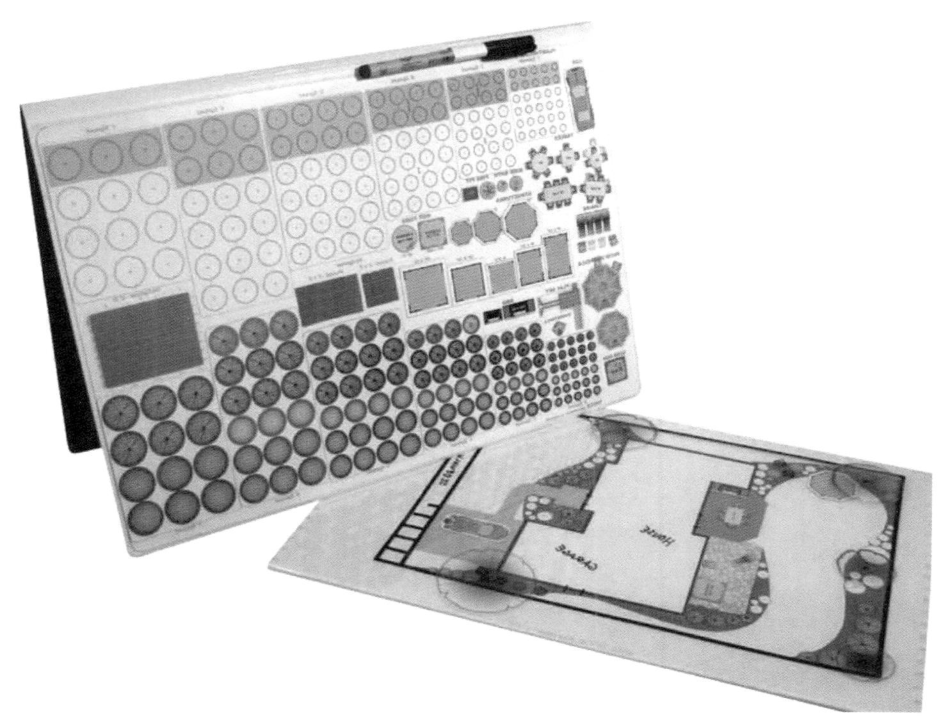

OutdoorKitchenDesignIdeas.com

Fetch-A-Sketch Outdoor Kitchen is a great source for design ideas and plans. Choose from hundreds of ready to use perspective drawings and construction plans. You can also shop for our top rated grills and accessories.

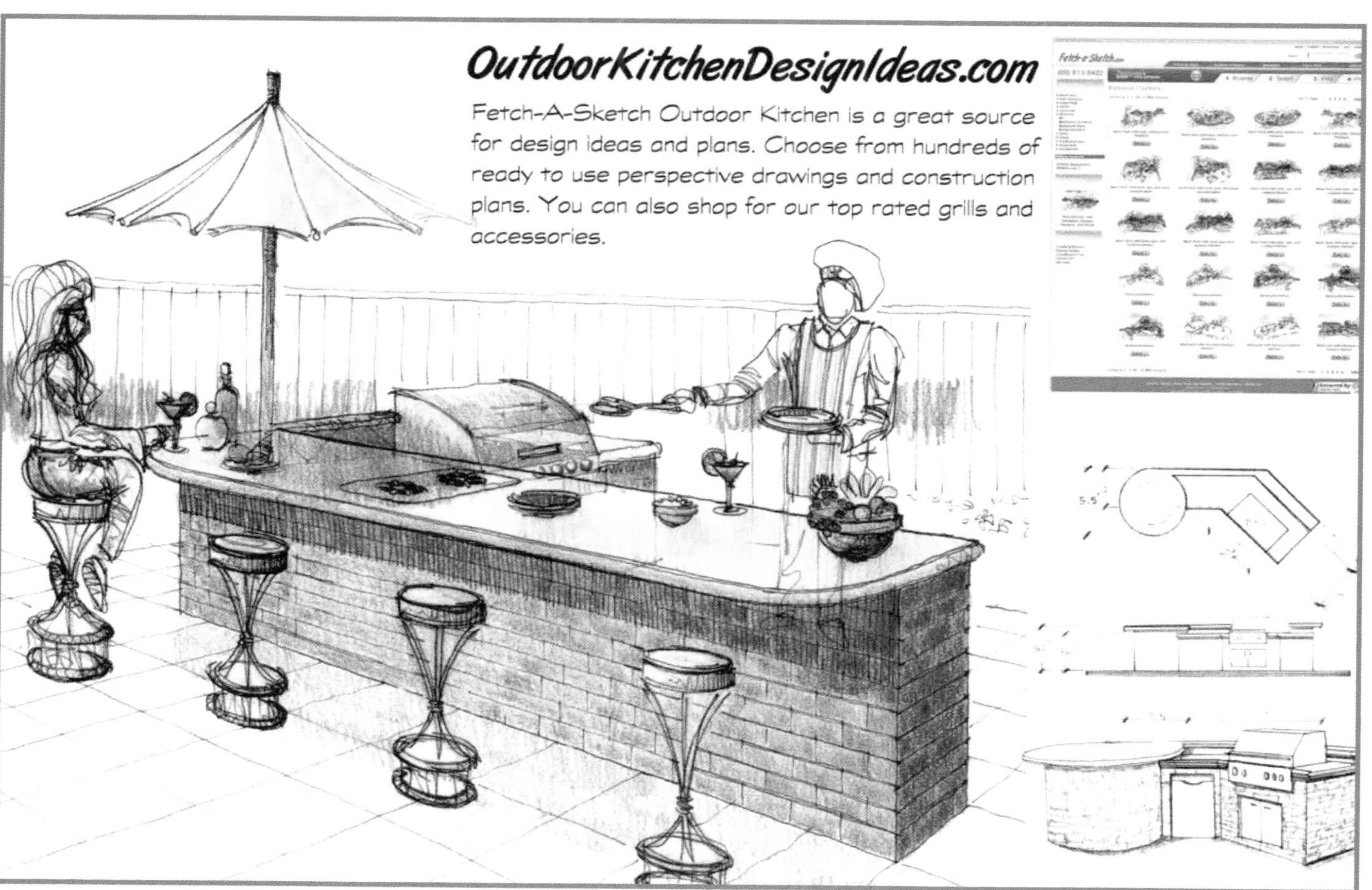

Eye Appeal: Flooring,

Countertops and More

Photo on these pages and preceding page by Deidra Walpole

Outdoor kitchens, dining rooms and living rooms make great companions outdoors. Nothing anchors the space of an outdoor living room with romantic ambience like a custom stone fireplace

Your outdoor kitchen plans are starting to come together. You have a location in mind, you know the appliances and accessories you want, and you have a pretty good idea of the layout. Now get ready for the really fun part. The flooring, countertops, and other creative elements of your new room will all help set the tone, define the style, and make the space uniquely and beautifully yours.

Photo by Deidra Walpole

The materials you choose offer countless ways to customize your outdoor kitchen. With different products and techniques, you can create an environment that reflects your own personal taste, whether it's elegant and sophisticated, artsy, whimsical, or just plain fun.

But the materials you use need to do more than just look good. They also need to function in ways that make your cooking and entertaining easier, more convenient, and even safer. Here's how to choose flooring and countertop materials that offer all of these qualities.

Flooring Fundamentals

A beautiful, functional kitchen really does start from the ground up. Choosing appropriate flooring will give you a long-lasting, great looking, trouble-free backdrop for all of your outdoor celebrations. Let's start with some options...

Option 1: Poured Concrete

One of the most affordable, versatile, and durable choices, concrete is also one of the most popular because of its endless design possibilities. It can be expertly colored, stamped, and finished in an infinite variety of textures and patterns - some that convincingly mimic real stone.

Patio Stamping Tip:
If you choose stamped concrete, take practical steps to make sure your outdoor floor lasts a long, long time. Select a stamp pattern that's not too deep to drain and that allows outdoor furniture to rest on it without leaning or wobbling.

Need a Second Opinion?
We always recommend consultation with a designer or contractor before you finalize your plans. The author regularly consults with homeowners, designers, and contractors.
Visit **ScottCohenDesigns.com** for a complete list of consultation services.

Option 2: Concrete Pavers

Today's manufactured concrete paving products come in an extensive array of colors, shapes, and surface textures to fit every décor, from old world to contemporary and cutting edge. Tumbled finishes capture the appearance of aged stone while pavers with smooth, crisp edges can be used for a more formal attitude. Pavers come in just about every color imaginable to reflect styles that are Mediterranean, Tuscan, French-country, Caribbean, Asian and everything in between.

Due to their thickness, concrete pavers offer high compressive strength–they are so strong, in fact, that they're commonly used for driveways. Because they are set in sand, pavers can also shift and move without cracking. This makes them a great choice for areas with clay soil that expands and contracts as moisture content varies. Pavers also offer an important environmental advantage in that they allow water to percolate through to the ground below, keeping rain water on site and out of storm-water systems. Finally, they can be easily lifted and replaced, allowing better access later on for utilities and repairs.

Many product lines include pavers of different shapes, colors, and sizes that are meant to be used together in one patio. They can be laid in decorative designs that incorporate borders, swirls, circular medallions, or fan arrangements or in patterns that appear completely random.

Option 3: Concrete Tile

Concrete tiles are another attractive option. These are wet-molded, shaped, and colored to mimic authentic cut stones that run the gamut in appearance from sleek to antique. Because they are created in molds, concrete tiles allow a more decorative textured surface than pavers, and they can be cast in any color we choose. Tiles can be created to replicate flagstone, slate, travertine, and cobblestone, yet they are much more resilient to changing weather conditions than their natural counterparts. They also offer superior slip resistance over ceramic tiles, making them a versatile, practical, and beautiful choice for outdoor rooms.

> **Tip:** Always make sure any flooring product you choose is specifically designed for outdoor use.

Option 4: Brick

Photo on these pages by Deidra Walpole

Brick is a truly timeless building material. These molded clay pavers have been used for literally thousands of years, and the look never goes out of fashion. Brick is especially suitable for a formal or classic design or for landscapes where the house itself incorporates brick.

When it comes to color, there's more than "brick red." Like the clay they are created from, bricks come in a diverse assortment of earth tones that naturally blend into an outdoor setting. This makes brick easy to coordinate with many color schemes.

Option 5: Natural Stone

For a head-turning outdoor floor with an organic aesthetic, natural stone is hard to beat. This is the real deal - the material that other products imitate (many do the job quite well). The soft colors of stone range from yellows, golds, and browns to reds and pinks, to blacks, blues, and even greens. While this palette isn't infinite, stone gives the designer plenty of possibilities.

The strength, texture, hardness, slip resistance, and maintenance requirements of each type of stone vary considerably. Some don't bear weight as well as others. Some are slippery when wet. Some stones are easy to seal; some are so porous that sealing is nearly impossible.

These differences count. For example, in the cooking area, the priority is for stone that is both slip-resistant and truly sealable. Therefore, if you're considering stone flooring, a trip to the stone yard to talk with an expert is in order. An expert can tell you what options are available and how they differ in appearance, texture, fade resistance, care required, and, of course, price.

Stone can be cut into irregularly shaped flat slabs, like flagstone, or in rectangles or squares, like slate. It can also be fabricated into consistently shaped tiles and pavers. The consistency of the shape, size, and thickness of your stone pieces will impact the look of the flooring and the labor and expertise required for installation.

Tip: All sedimentary rock, like slate and flagstone, will slough off in layers over time. This process is exacerbated by freeze-thaw cycles to the point that your patio may develop high or low spots. Keep this in mind when choosing patio materials for colder climates

This project was filmed over the course of a year for HGTV's "Get Out, Way Out!". Complete with outdoor kitchen, living room, covered dining room, and contemplation garden, it is easy to see why it is one of my favorites! The all-tile infinity edge pool took full advantage of the magnificent views from this backyard!

HGTV
Featuring Scott Cohen

Photo on these pages and preceding page by Deidra Walpole

Travertine: A Natural For Floors

Travertine, a natural sedimentary stone, is an attractive choice for outdoor flooring because of its warm color palette, its natural non-skid surface, its freeze-thaw resistance, and its rich, organic beauty. (Rome's Coliseum silently testifies to its durability.) Travertine pavers and tiles are both available, making it easy to coordinate counters with flooring. Travertine pavers are precisely cut to consistent dimensions so installation is similar to that of manufactured concrete pavers. Depending on the look you're seeking, you can find travertine pavers with a chiseled edge or with a tumbled finish for a more rough-hewn edge.

Mixing It Up

With so many great choices, it's easy to want them all. The good news is you don't have to limit yourself to one type of outdoor flooring. With thoughtful combinations and careful coordination, you can integrate several of your favorite choices into one cohesive design. In fact, mixing it up this way only enhances your outdoor room. Creative combinations enhance the outdoor room concept. Colors should always coordinate, but don't be afraid to stretch the boundaries of your imagination. For instance, in the project to the right, exposed aggregate flooring is used in the outdoor living room, tumbled concrete pavers for the outdoor kitchen, stamped concrete pads for the pathways, and wet set pavers for the sundeck.

Photo by Deidra Walpole

Soft Under Feet: Consider adding an area rug to your outdoor room. Rugs specifically designed for outdoor use are available in a wide selection of colors and patterns to accent your hardscape and outdoor furniture.

Even if you stick primarily with one material, you can mix colors and finishing techniques to define your spaces. For example, if you use poured concrete, you can apply different textures, stamp patterns, and finishes to give each area a slightly different feel. Stamping a pattern in a large circle, oval, or square can frame the kitchen area or give an area rug effect to an outdoor living room.

The use of steps to form height variations is another way to identify the transition between outdoor rooms. Step up to the barbeque, step down to the living room, step up to the fountain.

> Safety Tip: When adding a single step, be careful to place it where people expect it, so a step down doesn't become a tumble down. Signal the change in elevation by switching up materials or color of materials to trim a step.

Fetch-a-Sketch.com

Sorting Through Your Flooring Options

Sorting through all of your options can seem complicated at first. But there are a few basic considerations that will help you narrow your choices.

As with any building project, the adage "safety first" applies. To keep your guests upright and your cook cooking, choose flooring with slip and trip resistance in mind. Whether indoors or out, kitchens are always subject to spills, so slippery-when-wet is never a good quality for kitchen flooring. Natural stone pavers, concrete, and brick all offer feet a good grip, even when that spilled crushed ice lies melting on the floor.

Slipping is one thing, tripping is another. Outdoor parties are often held during evening hours, when the dimming light makes it harder to watch your step while carrying a tray from BBQ to dining table. While the uneven quality of some flooring materials, such as flagstone, can add rustic appeal, it may not be the best choice for pathways that are heavily traveled by family or guests in dim light.

Your Flooring Budget

Next to safety, budget usually plays a big role in flooring materials. A great way to stretch a flooring budget is to use more expensive materials like flagstone and brick as decorative trim. Just as you frame a picture, you can frame your patio with flagstone or brick or cast concrete. Then fill your field with a less expensive material, such as poured concrete, in a coordinating color. You don't have to choose the same materials as long as the ones you use provide some consistency in color and design.

Host Brandon Johnson of HGTV's "Get Out, Way Out!" followed Scott and The Green Scene construction crews from start to finish on this outdoor area built for family fun!

Flooring To Fit Any Style

- **Contemporary:** Slate or cast-concrete tiles; clean, washed concrete in integral colors
- **Tuscan:** Tumbled pavers, un-filled travertine, deep-washed exposed aggregate, or stone-texture stamped concrete
- **English/Traditional**: Brick, dark-hued flagstones, washed concrete, stamped cobblestone concrete
- **Tropical:** Flagstone, faux-rock texture-stamped concrete, wood decking
- **Old World:** Repurposed brick, exposed aggregate, Windsor cobblestone texture stamps, fleur-de-lis and grape vine borders.

Stamped & colored concrete: faux wood bridge and stone texture patio

Flooring Style Tip:
The style of your flooring should always coordinate with the overall theme or look you're trying to achieve in your yard. It should complement the home and the existing elements of your landscape. If your home includes brick architectural details, consider incorporating brick into your outdoor kitchen. If you've already used stone in other areas of your backyard, consider using it here too.

Protect Your Investment
To protect your gorgeous patios from oil and wine stains, consider applying a high quality penetrating sealer to any flooring in the cooking or dining areas. (See "Seal in the Beauty", page 127.) Some sealers can increase slipperiness, so be sure the product has an additive for slip resistance.

Stamped & colored concrete: stone texture patio

Tumbled concrete pavers with stamped & colored concrete band & poured in place concrete band

Flagstone with poured in place concrete band

Counter Intelligence

While the flooring you choose presents a beautiful backdrop for your outdoor kitchen, the countertops, backsplashes, and other decorative elements you choose offer an opportunity to create features that are as attractive as they are functional. Your counters are one place where your personality, taste, and imagination can really come alive.

For counter tops, the focus is on durability, weather resistance, ease of clean-up and maintenance, and, of course, stunning good looks. With a little planning and imagination you can design a counter with all of these qualities.

Casting Call

When it comes to creating countertops and other functional and decorative elements for the backyard barbeque, there are few materials I like better than cast concrete. Cast concrete is one of the fastest growing trends in outdoor kitchen design because of its natural beauty, versatility, its ability to withstand the elements, its structural integrity, and the complete design freedom it affords.

I can cast it into any shape. I can easily follow curves, integrate split levels, and incorporate decorative touches such as bull-nose, mantle, split-face stone, and rope edges. It can be colored and finished to reflect any style from clean and contemporary to tropical to old world Italian.

While countertops can be cast in a factory and then shipped to the site, I prefer to cast counters in place for outdoor kitchens. This process irons out the transportation and access issues associated with large pre-manufactured counters. There are no worries about how well it will ship, how you'll haul the heavy slab into place, or how well it will fit through the gate or other narrow spaces. Casting in place also allows us a lot more versatility when it comes to cantilevered edges, built-in patio cover posts and custom lighting effects.

With concrete we can easily sculpt motifs and patterns that reflect your hobbies or passions. A goblet and a cluster of grapes for a wine buff? You got it. A martini glass backsplash? No problem. How about a Japanese maple leaf mosaic backsplash for a Zen inspired garden?

Photo by Deidra Walpole

This unique Martini-themed swim-up outdoor bar and kitchen was featured on HGTV's Special Presentation "Big Splash". The tiles were custom-fabricated in my home ceramic studio. The clients and their children helped glaze the finished tiles (left).

For some real fun - and often dazzling results, cast concrete can be embedded with stones, mother of pearl, seashells or just about anything you like.

How about adding colorful sparkle to your kitchen by integrating crushed glass into a countertop honed to a smooth finish? Or take it up a notch by including some fiber-optic lighting underneath. That will really get things glowing.

As with any component of your outdoor kitchen, your counters need to be as functional as they are attractive. Cast concrete gets high marks here too. First of all it's extremely durable and can be formulated to accommodate any climate area. It will hold up to all the abuse a backyard cook can dish out – including piping hot pots and pans. It is easily cleaned and maintained.

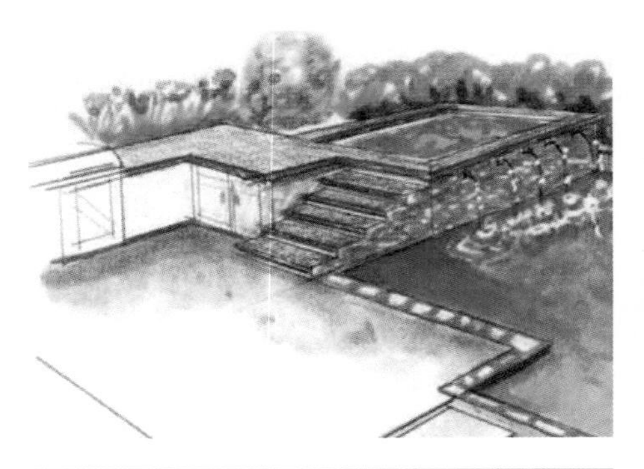

Tip: For extra durability we vibrate cast concrete into molds. This compresses it to remove tiny air pockets, resulting in a product that's three times as strong as it would be without this step. It also makes the surface more impervious to water. While a small amount of moisture is allowed to wick through, anything underneath the counter (such as your new stereo system) will stay dry and protected.

I made these whimsical three dimensional tiles in my home ceramic studio. To create the wine bottle tiles set in the counter, I melted full size bottles at 1450 degrees in my kilns. (Of course, I drank the wine first!)

A Greener Choice

Finally, cast concrete is gaining popularity as an environmentally efficient choice. The forms used are often reusable. Counters are built to the precise size needed so there is little waste. The cost and environmental impact of shipping are reduced because the counters are built on site. Best of all, when you imbed recycled objects like glass into cast concrete, you create gorgeous art out of materials that would otherwise go to the landfill.

Here is a small sample of the multitude of looks possible with a little concrete and a lot of imagination.

By hand-seeding a countertop with different materials, we make each one a unique, custom-crafted work of art.

Concrete Style

There was a time when the word concrete evoked images of cold, industrial gray. Those days are long gone. With a little color and a few finishing tricks, concrete can take on any personality. Here are some design ideas to fit your style:

Tuscan: Cast the concrete in tans and earth tones that match travertine colors. Use hand-seeded stone or hand-seeded stone combined with glass in shades of amber tan and brown.

English/Traditional: Use natural gray, bisque white or terra-cotta concrete colors with brick or cobblestone veneers.

Contemporary: Use un-tinted natural gray or bisque white. Incorporate square edges and clean lines. The addition of glass block provides modern architectural detail.

Tropical: Use natural colors. A rough hewn edge and free form design adds stone-age appeal. Incorporate stones used elsewhere in the yard into the counter design. Consider seeding with mother-of-pearl or seashells.

Understated Elegance: Hand seed with decorative pebbles. Cast in tans and brown and seed with smaller crushed glass in the same tones to give depth and sparkle.

Old World: Incorporate chiseled stone edge detailing cast in natural grey or sandstone colors with imbeds like pebbles in colors to match existing hardscape.

Whimsical: Hand seed with crushed glass in reds, yellows, and oranges or other vibrant shades. Embed objects that reflect your hobbies or theme. Consider adding fiber optic lighting from below. A sparkler wheel will set the design in motion.

More Options

Cast concrete isn't the only option for outdoor kitchen counters of course (even if it is my favorite). Ceramic tile, travertine, granite, slate, and many other natural stones also provide suitable choices for some kitchens and climates. Let's look at a few options.

Ceramic Tile

Ceramic tile has been a popular choice for counters indoors and out for many years. Tiles come in an unlimited selection of colors and patterns; they withstand heat; and they are relatively easy to wipe clean and care for. But be careful. It's critical to choose a tile that's rated for outdoor use. These tiles are typically very dense, have better impact resistance, and can withstand freeze-thaw cycles. Before making a selection it's important to consult with a knowledgeable distributor who can guide you on an appropriate tile choice that will suit your climate and the project. Consult with the manufacturer regarding installation materials and techniques to accommodate the outdoor environment.

Tip: Keeping your grout joints tight will ease clean-up and maintenance. Sealing with grout twice a year will keep those joints stain-free.

Stone And Stone Tiles

Natural stone counters are another option for higher-end kitchens. Granite, slate, soapstone, travertine, and marble are all used but not all are appropriate for every counter. Different stones have different hardness levels, porosity, and care requirements. Some types of stone may provide elegant, sophisticated beauty but come up short in a hardworking outdoor kitchen designed for frequent use. Be sure to consult an expert before choosing stone for your counters so you can be sure the strength, maintenance requirements, and other factors fit well with your own cooking style.

Tip: As with your outdoor flooring, be sure you understand and follow the sealing requirements for any outdoor counter. This will help keep your counters looking as good as they did the day they were installed.

Tip: If you like the look of stone or ceramic but don't want to give up the advantages of cast concrete, you can integrate stone or tile selectively in the backsplash or as part of an embedded pattern in your cast concrete counters.

Stone can be purchased as a single slab which gives a luxurious look and makes for easy, seamless cleaning. Some stone, such as slate and travertine, is also available as cut tiles which are installed much like ceramic tile.

A Well - Equipped Space

There are as many ways to outfit an outdoor kitchen as there are outdoor cooks. Your decisions should be based on how you cook and entertain, the kinds of foods you enjoy, and how creative you want to be with your outdoor dining events.

Photo by Deidra Walpole

Choose your options carefully. Remember that every item adds to the budget and takes up space. Many outdoor appliances require some maintenance (taking away from time you could spend enjoying the outdoors). If an appliance or accessory will get regular use, go for it. But if you think you'll only use it once a year (be honest here), save the space and simplify your life outdoors. Here's a rundown on the different appliances and accessories to consider.

The Leading Role: The Grill

In most outdoor kitchens, the grill takes center stage, so it's important to put a lot of thought into this decision. Here are some factors to consider:

Built-In Or Moveable

Grills are available as built-in or free-standing units. While outdoor kitchens are typically equipped with a built-in model, a free-standing, or cart-BBQ, makes sense in some cases, especially in sites where wind direction changes frequently. This way, when a strong wind makes cooking difficult, you can move the BBQ to the other side of the kitchen. Creating counters around a movable BBQ (top right) will give it the look and function of a built-in.

Size Matters

Yes, size does matter. Grills range in size from about 32" to a 52" monster. Many people assume a bigger one is always better. After all, a seemingly endless grilling surface equates to countless burgers for countless hungry partiers. If you've got the budget, why not go for it?

Well, before you do, consider this: First, the bigger the grill, the heavier it is to lift the hood. This can make it awkward for cooks of smaller stature to take a turn at the BBQ.

Second, the bigger the grill, the more space it takes up. If you have unlimited room, that might not be a big deal, but if space is at a premium, as it is in most kitchens, think carefully about how often you'll actually use that extra grilling surface. You may want to opt for more counter space instead.

Third, if you frequently cook for only two people, an over-sized hooded grill may not perform as well. A hooded grill is designed to rebound heat and focus it on the food. Most can't do the job as well if you're cooking a small amount of food in a cavernous space.

Outdoor Cooking Tip: Experience is the key. Keep a note pad handy to jot down notes (like how long it took to cook your meal and the cut and weight of the meat) for reference later. The more experience you have, the less time you will need to spend checking the grill. This is especially helpful with rotisserie cooking.

Once you've decided on an approximate size, it's time to think about accessories. Today's grills come equipped with a wide array of features to make your cooking more convenient and a lot more fun. Turn the page for a few suggestions.

Rotisserie: Gotta Have One

A rotisserie is a skewer that rotates the food over or next to the heat source. It's a must for any grill station. It's especially helpful when you're hosting company. Who wants to be a slave to the grill when you'd rather be spending time with your friends?

Rotisserie cooking allows you to prepare your dinner ahead of time. You can season your meat, heat the grill, and prepare the skewers all before company arrives. Once you actually start cooking, the rotisserie does the work and requires very little supervision. Finally, the food will almost always come out perfectly done, and you'll be the hero of the barbeque.

Rotisserie Trend:
New Alfresco models feature a powerful gear-driven motor hidden under the grill. No more motors hanging on the side of your grill exposed to the elements.

Photo by Deidra Walpole

Be sure to place an electrical outlet for the rotisserie motor. Most motors come with short cords so pay attention to which side of the grill the motor mounts and place the outlet accordingly. Some newer grill designs actually have gear or chain driven motors that plug in out of sight underneath the counter.

Consider a grill with rotisserie burners on the back side rather than below. Most high-end grills offer this option, which allows you to put a drip pan below your dinner to collect juices for basting or gravy. This way you don't have to deal with the flare ups that can occur when the heat source is from below.

Find Your Balance:
When prepping the food it's critical that the weight of the meat be centered on the skewer. Your food will cook more evenly and you won't burn out the rotisserie motor.

Photo by Patrick Stringer

Sear Zone

A sear zone (right) is a special burner that quickly reaches a very high heat – about 1400 degrees versus the 350-400 degrees of a typical burner. Searing uses this high heat to lock in the juices at the beginning of the cooking process. It's the secret to the succulent meats served at high end steak houses. When you sear meat, you cauterize it to keep the juices from escaping. After a quick sear, you can scoot the meat over to the other part of the grill to finish it off. Searing is also a great way to prepare a perfect ahi tuna steak without overcooking the inside - a feat that's nearly impossible on a regular BBQ burner.

Steamer /Fryer

These deep outdoor cookers (right) are great for fish fries, onion rings, lobster boils, or even for deep frying a whole turkey. These are available either as drop-in or stand-alone units.

Smoker Drawer/Smoker Box

Want smoky applewood flavor with the convenience of a gas grill? Consider a smoker drawer. This small drawer, tray or box can be filled with wood chips (wet or dry) to add a variety of smoky flavors to your gas grilling.

Teppan Grill

Teppan grills are one of the latest outdoor kitchen trends. Teppanyaki, a traditional Japanese cuisine prepared using a large iron griddle, has evolved in the US into a lively form of dinner entertainment. The skilled teppan chef takes center stage and works magic, typically with a variety of meats and an array of vegetable accompaniments.

Placing your teppan griddle in the center of a dining table or counter will add great entertaining value to the outdoor kitchen. They come in numerous sizes in square or circular shapes to fit most counter and tabletop configurations. In addition to the cuisine teppan chefs made famous, the addition of one of these large griddles to your outdoor kitchen can bring pancake breakfasts, after-dinner crepes, grilled cheese sandwiches, or panini to your backyard cooking.

Tip: A teppan grill can double as a hot plate, essentially giving you two appliances in one space.

Keep It Clean:
Here are a few tips on how to keep those beautiful stainless steel appliances looking new. Simple Green® Stainless Steel One-Step Cleaner & Polish works well and is easy to use. Other, less expensive options include warm water or a mild detergent. Wipe in the direction of the polish lines and towel dry. You can also use household solutions such as ammonia or vinegar. Apply with a clean spray bottle and wipe dry with a soft cloth. Whichever method best suits you, remember to wipe in the direction of the polish and dry thoroughly.

Warming Drawers

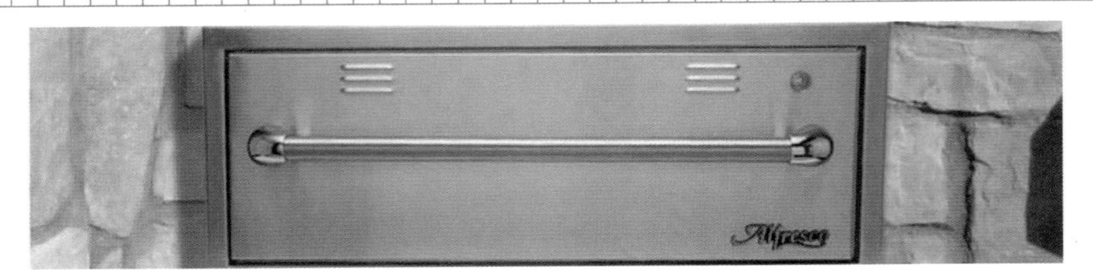

These stainless steel, under-counter drawers (right) offer another way to heat up side dishes or keep food warm until everyone's ready to eat. When they're not used for food, they're a great way to keep those pool towels luxuriously warm.

Side Burner

Whether you're boiling the corn, heating the beans, or making the bourbon-mustard reduction sauce to go with your grilled pork chops, having a side burner (right) nearby can be pretty handy. Think carefully about the way you BBQ before you include one though. Some outdoor cooks hardly ever use their side burners. Others wouldn't cook without one...or even two.

Hot Plate

These are used primarily for keeping food hot for large groups. Note that these electric appliances can use up a lot of amperage. Be sure your outdoor kitchen has an additional dedicated breaker if you intend to use these types of appliances.

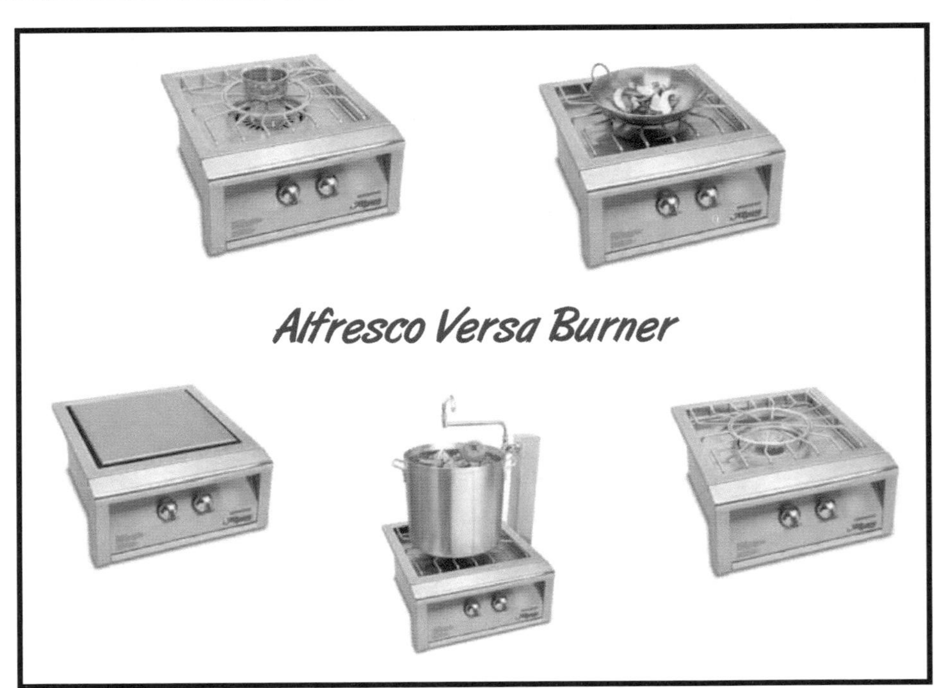

Alfresco Versa Burner

BBQ Lighting

Lighting is available inside many high-end grills so you can always see what you're cooking. (Sorry, no more excuses for burning the food after dark.)

Wok Burner

A wok burner truly blends the indoor kitchen with the outdoor cook top. Wok burners have been a feature in cart barbecues for many years, so the addition of a wok burner to an outdoor kitchen is an obvious choice. Even if you're not barbecuing, the outdoor wok can make cooking during warmer months a much cooler experience.

Bar Fridge

An outdoor fridge or wine chiller (or beer chiller for those who prefer fermented hops to fermented grapes), can eliminate walking back and forth to the indoor kitchen for cold food or drinks. But if you plan to use it primarily for beverages, consider this: Most guests feel free to reach into a cooler to help themselves to a cold one but often hesitate to open the closed door of a fridge. And remember, a refrigerator burns a lot of energy year-round. Unless you'll regularly use it for outdoor food prep or to store pre-prepared platters of meat, consider skipping the fridge to save space for something else, such as...

Beverage Center

A dedicated beverage center is an inviting option for serving drinks. These can be simple or elaborate, from a stainless steel drop-in cooler that includes condiment trays to a full-service cocktail station that includes everything you need to serve drinks in style: a faucet and sink, ice bin, under-counter bottle storage, cutting board, bottle opener, towel bar, and drop-in ingredient center. Removable bins make for easy cleanup. Plan for a drain below so that when ice melts it flows out of the counter area.

Storage Drawers And Doors

Cupboards and drawers are great storage additions to the outdoor kitchen, separating the BBQ 'tools of the trade' from the indoor kitchen essentials. These storage spaces are generally made from stainless steel.

Removable drawers can be used for food preparation.

Sink

For some, an outdoor kitchen wouldn't be complete without a sink for cleaning up. Install one in your outdoor kitchen and you may never cook inside again. (Hint: this is a great way to get the kids interested in helping with the dishes.) Check with local building codes. Some communities require expensive sewer connections for outdoor sinks.

Griddle Plate

This flat hot plate can be inserted over a side burner. It's an inexpensive way to achieve some of the same cooking benefits of a teppan grill. You can cook veggies to perfection without having to worry about them falling through the grill.

Tip: Most outdoor griddles should be oiled and covered when not in use to protect them from the elements.

Recycling Tip Include two thru-counter chutes and identify one for recyclables and one for trash or make a round chute opening for bottles and cans.

Trash/Recycling Receptacles

Make sure to dedicate space under the counter to hide the trash and recyclables you'll generate during your outdoor events. Thru-counter trash chutes and pull-out trash bins work well.

Plating & Garnish Center

If you're a big time entertainer, consider a plating and garnish station to create food presentations like a pro. These restaurant-inspired stations hold plates and a number of garnishes with room to put it all together in style.

Photo by Deidra Walpole

Pizza Oven

Clients frequently ask about pizza ovens. An outdoor, wood-fired brick oven can be an attractive, useful addition for a true chef who really has the time and inclination to use it for more than just cooking pizza. But when people find out that it takes about two hours to pre-heat a brick oven, they soon realize it's not for their quick weeknight pizzas. The fact is, many of these pizza ovens sit unused for months at a time. They're nice to look at, but if you're going for looks, why not save your money and space for something else – like an old-world stone fireplace you can cozy up to on any night of the week.

Brick ovens are for cooks with time and inclination to cook much more than just pizza.
photo courtesy of www.harmonyoutdoorliving.com

What Every Kitchen Needs

While most outdoor kitchens won't have all of these components, there are a few items (big and small) that no outdoor kitchen should be without. These include:

- ☑ Grill
- ☑ Rotisserie
- ☑ Counter space for food prep and setting trays down
- ☑ Storage space
- ☑ Trash containment system
- ☑ Cutting board
- ☑ Towel rack and/ or paper towel holder
- ☑ Beverage serving station
- ☑ And don't forget the bottle opener

Construction Techniques: Cast-In-Place Concrete Counters

Because of its beauty, durability, and unlimited design potential, cast-in-place concrete is my top choice for durable and easy-care outdoor counters. Concrete counters do not have the many grout lines that tile counters are plagued with. The lack of grout lines makes concrete counters easier to seal and keep clean than tile. Unlike granite it can be cast in any shape without seams. It can also be formulated to withstand freezing better than granite.

The following pages outline some special techniques for creating gorgeous, durable counters with concrete.

Assess Your Ability

These techniques require advanced masonry experience and skills. Before taking on a project of this scale, make sure you have those skills. Otherwise, call a concrete contractor. You can find one online at: ConcreteNetwork.com

Note: The following is a step-by-step construction method we use here in sunny Southern California, in a mostly non-freezing zone. Soils types, weather conditions, and building and safety codes vary greatly from region to region so be sure to consult your local permit office or a structural engineer to find out whether our method will work for your application.

Step 1: Stub Utilities

Run your gas, electric and drainage lines to the counter location and stub out for future tie-ins.

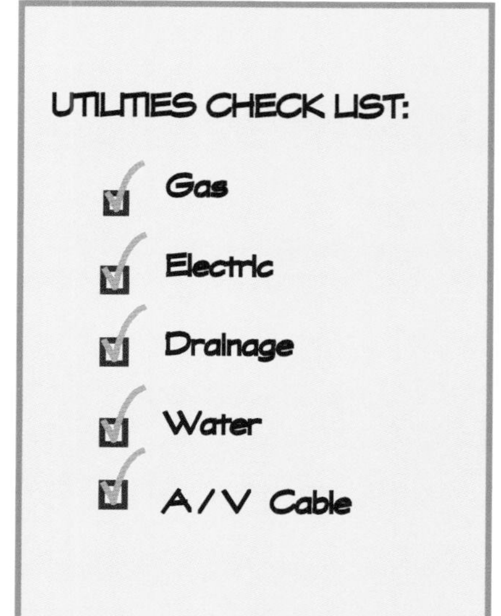

Step 2: Pour Footing

Excavate soil to allow for a 12 to 18-inch deep concrete footing. Consider your soil type, local codes, size of counter and depth of cantilever to help determine how large the footing should be. If you are not familiar with calculating loads, it's a good idea to consult with a local structural engineer or architect to help design your footing and structural steel detail.

Set rebar steel reinforcement to support your counter walls and tie into the footing.

Drainage Note:
To make clean-up and maintenance easy, always place a few drains in the concrete floor near your counters and pitch your concrete toward the drains. When routinely cleaning your outdoor kitchen, you can simply hose out under the counter.

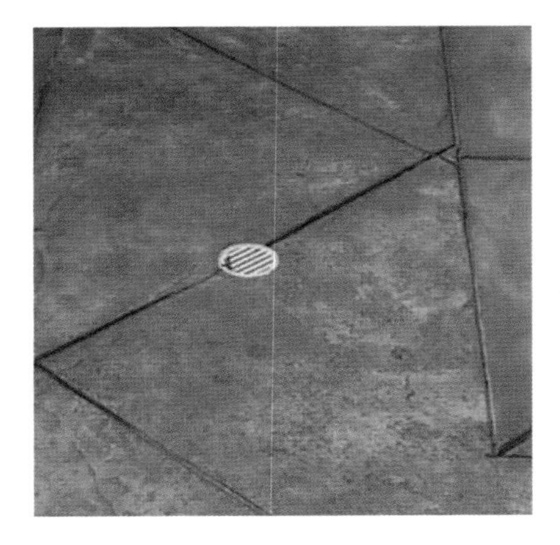

Step 3: Stack Walls

Set your cinderblocks over rebar steel reinforcement. We grout our walls solid (by filling all the cinderblock cells with concrete), so there is no need to grout between each course of block.

Set the steel in place for cantilevers.

Step 4: Install Counter Form Support

Create the bottom of the counter with either concrete board or plywood. We prefer to use concrete board in hard-to-reach areas so we can leave it in place. If you use plywood forms, you'll need to remove them because the wood will rot over time.

When wrapping a post always use expansion foam

Step 5: Place Edge Forms And Add Release Agent

Use wooden 2 x 4's on edge to support Styrofoam edge forms. Use screws – not nails – to set your forms, because you will need to remove the edge forms during the finishing process without disrupting your bottom forms.

Step 6: Add Steel And Reinforcement

Concrete countertops are basically "bridges" between two walls. As such, the stress point on the concrete is toward the bottom of the slab and not in the middle, like it is when we pour driveways and patios. Steel reinforcement should be placed in the bottom third of the slab. We use steel welded wire mesh with a 4" x 4" grid as our first choice. Rebar is used for cantilever support and backsplash tie-in. Sizing of the rebar is determined by a structural engineer or architect.

Mix the desired concrete color and pour your concrete counter with a 6.5 sack concrete mixture and a very low water ratio.

Shade your work area with a tarp or "Easy-Up" type structure to keep the counter out of full sun. This will prevent your concrete from setting-up prematurely.

Consolidated concrete is denser and less porous resulting in less shrinkage cracks and improved stain resistance. On most projects I use an integral colored concrete mixture (Davis brand Sandstone and Adobe are the most popular).

Step 8: Consolidate Concrete With Vibration

Use a concrete vibrator to work the edges along your forms and pass through the field of concrete. Vibration consolidates the concrete by removing air gaps and settling the aggregate. The result is a denser concrete with increased strength and waterproofing qualities.

Be careful not to overdo the vibration process or all of your large aggregate will settle to the bottom of your casting, while the water will come to the top. This can result in a crazed surface filled with hairline cracks. It can also result in a weak counter that may delaminate in sections later on. One pass of the vibrator is adequate to get all of the benefits from the tool.

Step 9: Float Concrete

Using a wooden trowel, smooth out the concrete inside your forms.

Step 10: Edge The Forms

Using a steel edging tool, work the outer perimeter of the forms.

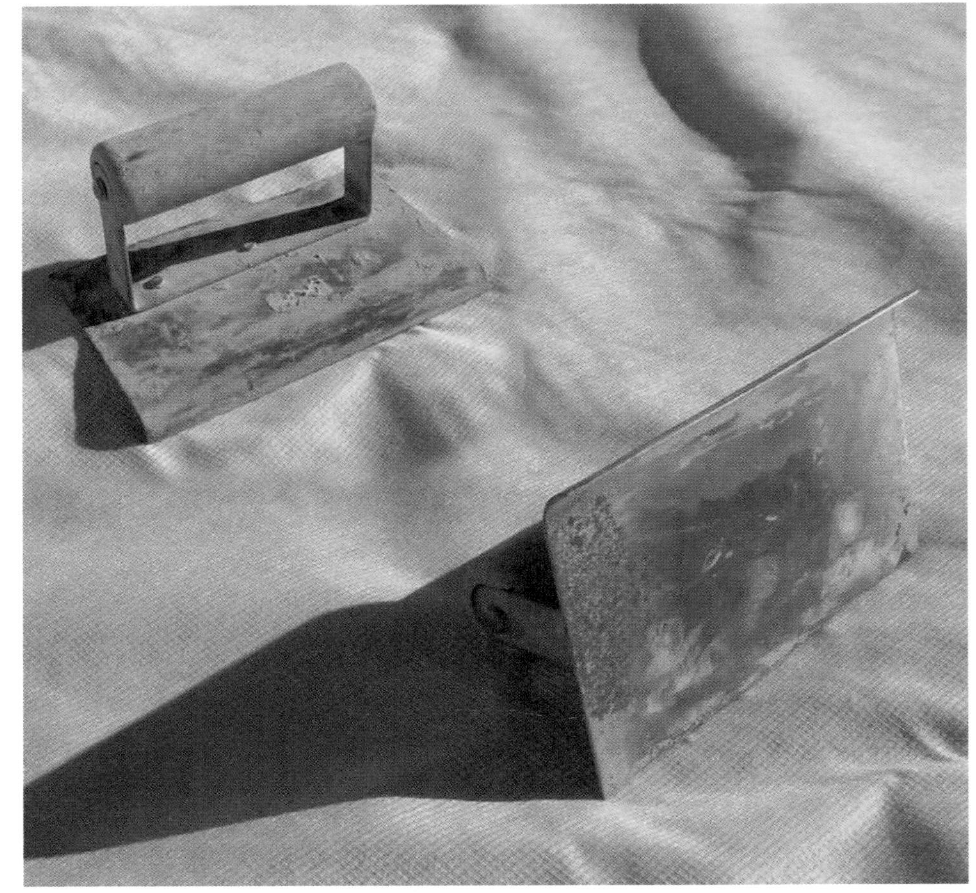

Step 11: Finish The Top

After the bleed water has dried from the surface, finish the top with a steel trowel until it's smooth. Don't overdo this step or you can burn, mar, or scare the surface.

Step 12: Clean the Edges

Pull the edge forms and clean up the edges with a sponge or matching edge-finish tool.

Step 13: Pull Bottom Forms

Wait 7 to 10 days before pulling the forms from cantilevered areas or the bottom of the counter. Strip the forms and haul away the debris.

Step 14: Cure The Counter

Allow the counter to cure for 7 to 28 days depending on the final finish desired. If you are going to polish the counter, get on it a little earlier, around 7 to 10 days. If you are just going to lightly wet sand the top, wait the full 28 days.

Step 15: Wet The Sand

Our standard finish includes a couple of hours of wet sanding with a hand held vibrating sander and a 400 grit wet sandpaper. This process allows us to clean up edge details and smooth the counter surface. Be careful not to overdo the sanding unless you desire a surface that shows the sand and aggregate in the countertop.

Step 16: Seal The Counter

Follow the guidelines on the next page to seal in the beauty of your new concrete countertop.

Tip: Avoid glaring errors. Be careful when using high gloss sealers outdoors. Blinding sunlight bouncing off the counter can be very annoying. While I sometimes use a high gloss sealer to show off the colors of a countertop in the shade, I never use anything higher than medium gloss for counters in the sun.

Seal in the Beauty: Sealers Protect Your Investment

To maintain the beauty of your cast concrete counters and floors you'll want to choose an appropriate, high quality sealer. There are many types of sealers and they are not all the same. Each is formulated with different ingredients. These ingredients have different properties and perform different functions.

A good sealer will help protect concrete from stains and etching while resisting scratches, heat, and UV degradation. Ideally it will be simple to apply and maintain and will help make clean-up in your outdoor kitchen much easier. Some sealers also enhance the appearance of concrete, giving it a richer, more saturated color or a higher gloss. No sealer does all of these jobs perfectly. Many perform well at some jobs (like stain resistance) and not-so-well at others (like ease of application). This doesn't mean they are bad products - just that not all products are right for every application. To choose the best sealer or sealers for your project, first determine the functions and properties that are most important to you. Then look for products specifically formulated to meet your expectations. Ask the manufacturer, dealer, or your contractor how the sealer you're considering meets the following criteria:

- Stain resistance - How impervious is the formula to stains? Does it completely block food stains or simply buy you some time and make spills easier to clean?
- Etch resistance - How will the product react to acids spills like lemon juice and vinegar? Acid will strip some sealers leaving the underlying concrete vulnerable to etching.
- Scratch resistance - Does the sealer scratch easily? Some do and must be frequently repaired.
- UV stability - Is the project located in sun or shade? Some sealers discolor or break down when exposed to sunlight.
- Heat resistance - What will happen if you set a hot pan down on the concrete? Heat will mar or even melt some sealers.
- Ease of application, maintenance, and repair - Can you apply the product yourself? How long will it take? How many steps are involved? Will you need to reapply frequently? Can you repair any problems? Be realistic about the amount of time you're willing to put into maintaining your sealer.
- Appearance - Do you want to keep the exact look of the unsealed concrete or would you like a deeper color or higher sheen? Some products darken the concrete slightly giving it a "wet" look. Some provide a medium or high gloss. Epoxy sealers create a plastic-like sheen over the entire surface.

So many sealers...

There are two main types of sealers: penetrating and topical. Penetrating sealers actually soak into bare concrete while topical sealers create a film or barrier on the surface.

Penetrating

Penetrating sealers help keep substances from readily soaking into the concrete. While they don't actually block spills from making contact with the concrete, they make cleaning up spills easier and give you more time to catch them before they stain. Because they don't provide long-term stain protection or significant protection against acids like vinegar and lemon juice (which can etch unprotected concrete), they are best for applications that won't be subject to frequent food spills or delayed clean-ups.

Continued

More on Sealers:
Among penetrating sealers, different products work in different ways. Some actually harden the concrete or decrease its porosity while others cause spills to bead up preventing them from soaking in. Many do not change the appearance of the bare concrete in any way. Others can be used to enhance the concrete, giving it a slightly darker or wet look.

Topical
Topical sealers generally form a protective layer on the surface of the concrete. There are several types of topical sealers and each has its own strengths and weaknesses.

Wax as a sealer is very easy to apply and maintain but it must be frequently reapplied to provide any protection at all. It doesn't hold up well to scratches or acid spills and it provides little stain protection. Because it is not heat resistant, wax isn't practical for counters that will serve as a landing zone for hot pots. On the positive, wax sealers can enhance the beauty of concrete by darkening it and adding a moderate to high sheen. Their ease of application is another plus.

Acrylic sealers are also easy to apply and these offer more stain protection and better heat resistance than wax. They are also UV stable. Acrylics are available either as solvent based lacquers that provide a wet, glossy finish or as water-based sealers that result in a dry, natural surface. Acrylics can scratch easily and must sometimes be repaired. This can be challenging with water based acrylics but with solvent based sealers, touch-ups are easy.

Urethane sealers have excellent stain resistance and heat resistance but are more complex to apply. They require meticulous surface preparation and many require mixing two parts. If you do it right, urethane will perform extremely well. However, if these steps are not done correctly, you can greatly increase the chance of product failure.

Epoxy is another type of topical sealer that is complicated to apply but provides excellent stain protection. Epoxies include two substances that react together when mixed to form a tough, durable coating. The result is usually a thick, high gloss surface with a plastic-like sheen. This sheen doesn't appeal to everyone so be sure to look at a sample before selecting this. Epoxies are not UV stable and can yellow and degrade in sunlight unless a UV inhibitor is added.

Take a look at your own priorities to determine which sealer will keep your cast concrete looking its best. For example, completely blocking stains may not be as important to you as protection from hot pots and pans. Scratch resistance may not be important if the product is easy to apply and repair. UV resistance may be a non-issue of the counter is located in the shade.

The Best Of Both Worlds
As you can see, there is no perfect sealer. Both topical and penetrating sealers have advantages and disadvantages. To provide the most thorough protection we typically use both a penetrating and a topical sealer. We first apply the penetrating sealer to increase the hardness and density of the concrete. Then we apply a lacquer type topical sealer over it to enhance the beauty and provide long term stain protection.

Construction Techniques: Cast Countertops With Embeds

The popularity of cast concrete outdoor kitchen counters continues to grow at a rapid rate. The ease of maintenance, ability to withstand the elements and versatility are certainly contributing factors, but I believe it is the beautiful rich look that has given concrete counters the lift to fame. Here are some tips on choosing the right colors and hand-seed embeds to create a one-of-a-kind art piece in your own backyard.

Variations in the use of glass chips in decorative concrete are limited only by your imagination. How the glass is applied, the quantities of glass used, chip size and the mixes of colors chosen can provide a unique signature product for those up to the challenge.

For more glass combination ideas visit OutdoorKitchenDesignIdeas.com

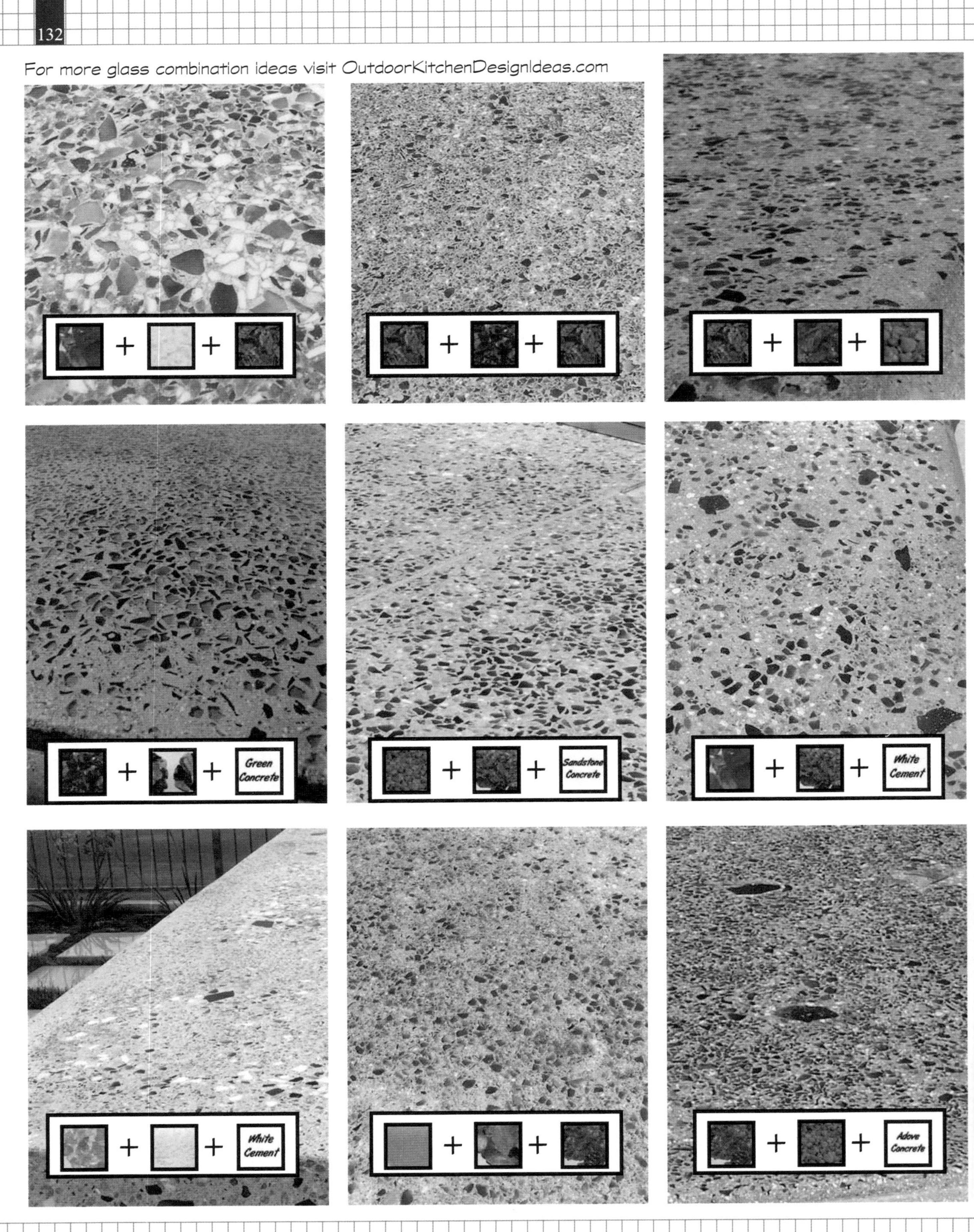

Seed or Mix?

Glass can be added to concrete counters by either (1) seeding the surface or (2) mixing the glass chips integrally.

"Seeding" glass means sprinkling, or spreading the glass onto the surface of the concrete after the concrete has been placed into the counter mold. The advantages of seeding glass is that you use a lot less glass compared to mixing integrally and you have more control over placement of different colors and mixes. The disadvantage to hand seeding is that it is tricky to uniformly spread the glass and it requires a more experienced masonry finisher to produce a quality piece. I prefer hand seeding because of the versatility it gives me with color blending:

Step 1: Make The Mold

Prepare your countertop mold and apply release agent to the forms.

If you want glass presence in the edge details, toss glass chips up against your edge forms before placing concrete.

Step 2: Pour & Vibrate

Place your concrete mixture into molds and lightly vibrate the forms and concrete to consolidate the concrete.

Tip: Add an acrylic fortifier to your mix. Use of an acrylic fortifier to the concrete mix helps glass chips adhere to the concrete. Acrylic fortifiers also improve resistance to water penetration

Step 3: Rough Finish

Bull float the concrete to smooth out the surface, but don't rough trowel or finish trowel just yet.

Step 4: Seed The Glass

Spread the glass out evenly on your concrete surface using whatever quantity, colors, and mixes you desire. If you are using varying size glass chips, apply the larger sizes first, then apply the medium chips and finish off with the smaller chips.

Step 5: Tamp & Trowel

Carefully tamp the glass down into the top surface of the concrete mixture with a wood float. Lightly trowel the glass into the concrete, gently pushing the glass into the still wet mixture until all glass is covered with the cementitious cream. Take care not to push the glass too deep into the mixture or you will have an uneven glass presence and the grind, hone, and polishing process can take much longer

Step 6: Cure The Concrete

Allow the concrete to cure for approximately 7 to 14 days depending on atmospheric conditions.

Attempting to finish the surface too early will damage the surface and send glass chips flying. Finishing the surface too late will take much longer and will put undue wear on your finishing tools. Any cure time between 7 and 28 days is acceptable.

Step 7: Grind, Hone & Polish

Heavy-duty polishing tools are equipped with progressively finer grits of diamond-impregnated pieces or disks (similar to sandpaper). These gradually grind down the surface until the desired amount of glass and stone is revealed.

I prefer to use a multi-head polisher rather than a single head polisher for a swirl-free finish on the top surface. Wet grinding, sanding, and polishing reduces the amount of dust you will be exposed to compared with a dry grinding process. Take time with each progressive level of sanding using finer and finer grits until the sheen you desire is accomplished.

Tip:
Be patient with each level of polishing grits. If you rush to the next finer grit too soon you'll burn through those expensive diamond tipped polishing pads too quickly.

Step 8: Seal the Surface

After allowing the counter to cure at least 28 days and dry completely from the polishing process, apply the sealer, or combination of sealers, that best suits your needs.

See page 127 for information on sealing.

Tip:
If you seal before the counter is completely dried out, a milky cloudiness can appear below the sealer and taint the appearance of your finished piece.

Pebbles

Seashells

Endless Edge Details
There are many Styrofoam forms that are inexpensive and easy to use to create a wide variety of different edge details. Granite edge details get expensive when thicker than 1 inch.

There are many inexpensive and easy to use Styrofoam forms available for creating a wide variety of different edge details. They can be purchased ready to use from masonry supply shops like "ArrowTool.com" or "Stagmeir", or custom made for you by a local foam cutting shop.

Mantle Edge Form

Square Edge

Upside Down Mantle Edge

Rope Edge

Note:
The form used here is rubber, not Styrofoam.

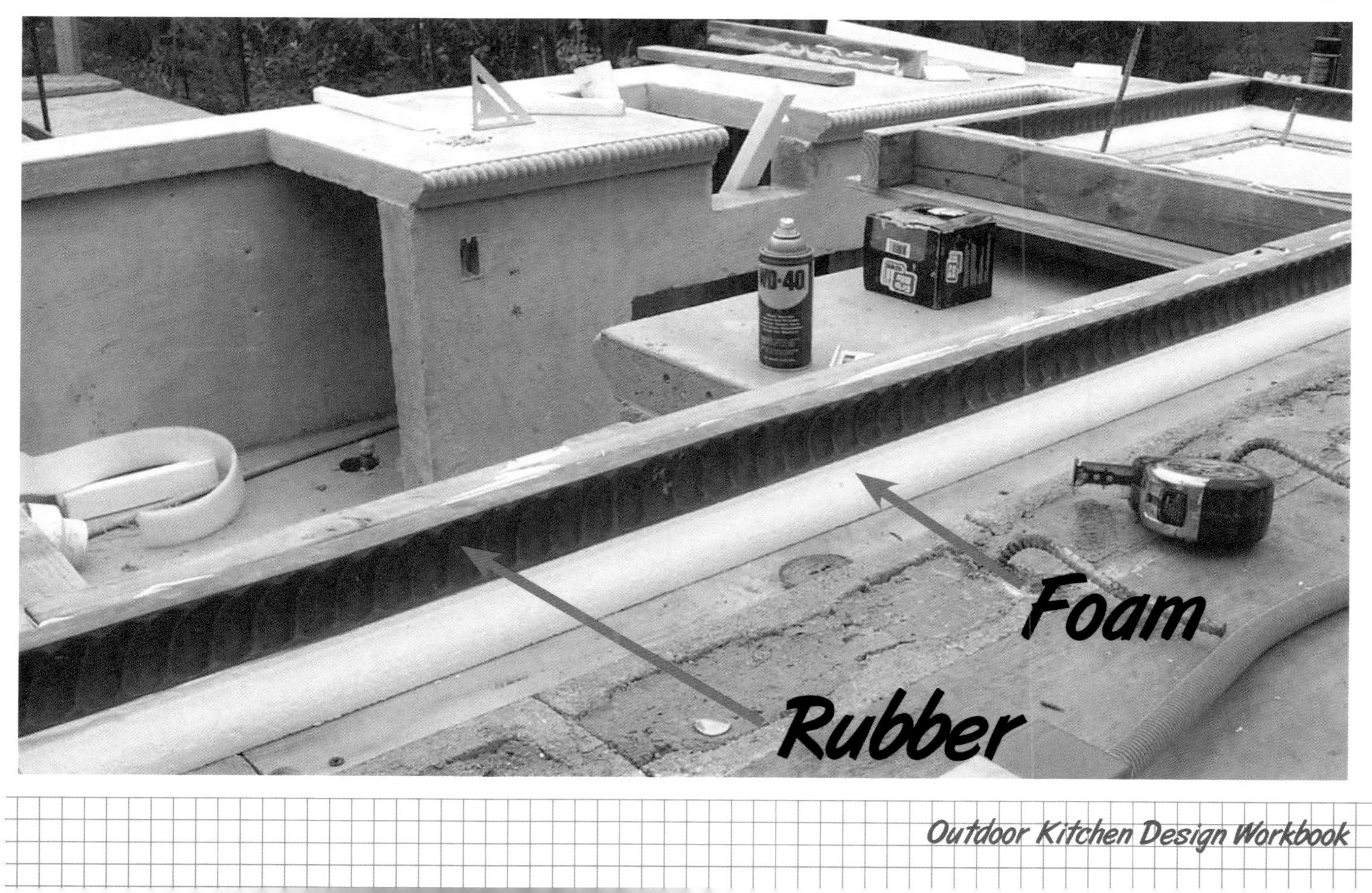

HGTV
property BUZZ

Fetch-a-Sketch.com
Scott Cohen

Catch the Glow: Add Lighting To Your Cast Glass Counters With Fiber Optics

Outdoor kitchens are all about entertaining, good dining, and alfresco fun! One of my favorite outdoor kitchen secrets is building counters that come to life at night with the help of fiber-optic lighting cables. These cables can be cast directly into the concrete for fascinating effects limited only by your imagination. Use these examples and instructions as a guideline to help create your own party focal point.

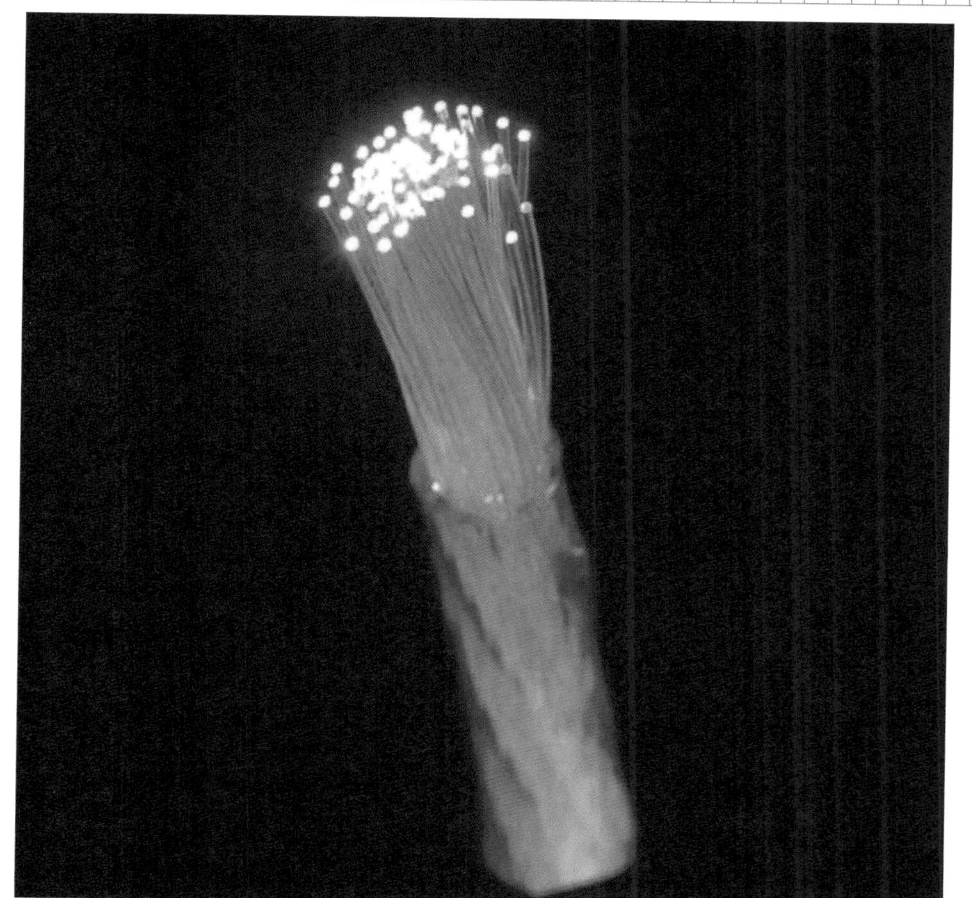

What Are Fiber Optics?

You hear about fiber optics whenever people talk about telephone lines, television cable and the Internet. Fiber optic lines are thin strands of optically pure glass or plastics that are capable of carrying light and/or digital information over long distances.

For our purposes, we will deal with just the light-carrying properties of fiber optics. Light in a fiber optic cable travels through the core by constantly bouncing back and forth. This allows the cables to bend and curve and still carry light from the main source of illumination.

What Is An Illuminator?

An illuminator is the source of the light. It's basically a box with a bright halogen light and a bundle of cables held in place directly in front of the bulb. The bright white light is carried down the cables to create hundreds of points of light from just the one bulb. A typical illuminator will hold 250-350 fibers depending on how thick the fiber strands are.

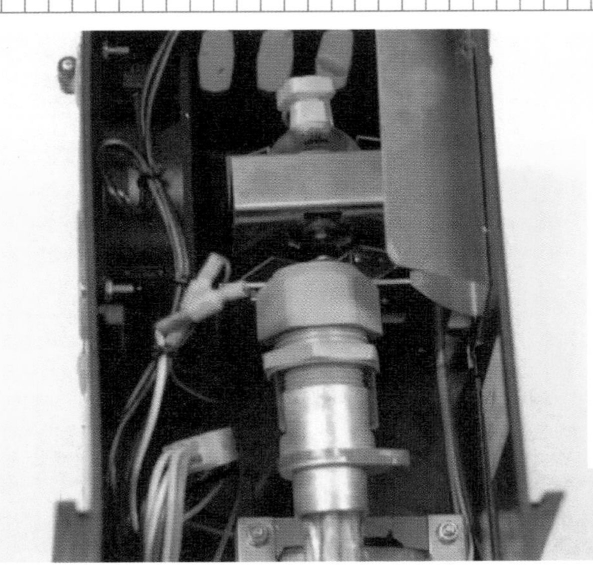

Illuminators and sparkler wheels are available from pool supply companies or online.

For even more interest, illuminators are available with a "color wheel" or a "sparkler wheel". Color wheels spin slowly in front of the white light bulb and change the color of light at the end of the fibers. They come standard with green, blue, magenta, and white color, but can be special ordered in custom color blends if you desire. Sparkler wheels can be used to create a twinkling "starry sky" effect. As the sparkler wheel turns, it varies the amount and location of the white light so the fiber ends fade and glow like the starry skies. The effect is both subtle and enchanting.

Before You Begin

When constructing a concrete counter with fiber optic lights, the first step is to determine the location of the illuminator and the amount of cables required to create the desired effect. In most cases, I place the illuminator directly below the counter to reduce the length of the expensive fiber-optic cables. Illuminators can overheat and burn out the bulbs prematurely, so be sure to add a screened vent under the counter to ensure adequate airflow.

These photos demonstrate down lighting

A Subtle Approach

There are two primary approaches to lighting counters with fiber-optics. One is to place the cables through the finished surface so that at the end of the polishing process you can easily see the points of light at the end of the exposed cables. While this results in points of light that can easily be seen, the lights can sometimes shine directly into the viewers' eyes for an undesirable effect. Instead, I prefer to glue the ends of the cables to chunks of glass in order to defuse the light and give the counter a more subtle glowing effect.

Step 1: Form The Counter

Set your forms in place and prep the counter as described previously.

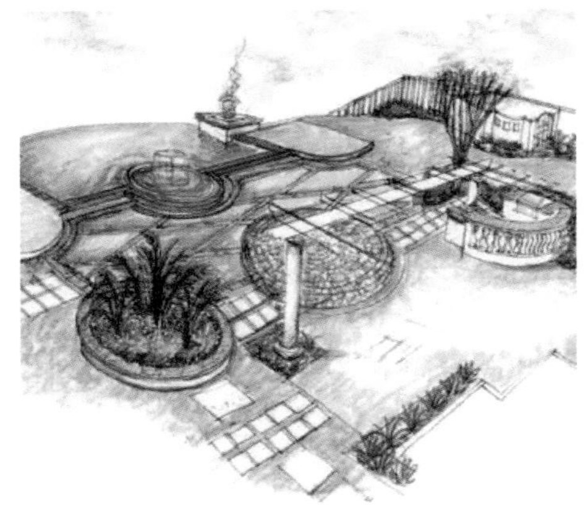

Step 2: Glue Cables To Glass Chunks

Run fiber-optic cables up through the bottom of the forms and spread out the ends of the cables at random. Smash the ends of the cables with a hammer or other blunt object to fray and roughen them. This process helps the cables stick to the glass chunks and also diffuses the light at the end of the strand. Using a hot glue gun, attach strands of cable to chunks of glass. Use one to two cables for lighter colored or smaller chunks of glass; use two to four cables for darker or larger chunks of glass.

Step 3: Set Cabled Glass At Finish Height

Using a very dry, low slump concrete mixture (with acrylic fortifier), place the cabled chunks of glass on cones of concrete just slightly higher than the counter finish height. Repeat the process until all glass chunks are set securely in place. Take care to place the glass randomly, unless a more structured, formal pattern is desired.

Step 4: Cast The Concrete Counter

Pour and cast the counter as described in Basic Techniques: Cast In Place Concrete. Vibrate the edges.

Step 5: Cure Concrete

Allow the concrete counter to cure for 7-18 days.

Step 6: Grind Off Excess Glass

Using a single head grinder, remove the excess glass above the finish grade of the counter. This step will save you hours of polishing and excess wear on your tools.

Step 7: Finish Up

Grind, hone and polish the counter to the desired finish

Intertool 3 head polisher

Step 8: Seal The Counter

For easy cleaning and durability, follow the guidelines on page 127 to seal your beautifully illuminated counter.

Original Works Of Art

On this very custom counter I personally hand-seeded glass beads to mimic grapevines. Over 900 fiber-optic cables underneath fed the grapevine, and the counter was connected to a special order illuminator. Every couple of minutes the light would dart up the length of the vine with over 200 hand-placed cables for a shooting star effect. The remainder of the counter featured 700 additional cables that sparkled like a starry night. The completed project took 6 weeks to build and was one of my personal best.

An Important Word To Contractors: Part of the magic of this technique is the fact that it always results in a unique, original work of art. The variability of the recycled glass pieces and curve of each set of cables means the effects will vary from piece to piece. This is art and the old expression "it's not cast in stone" does not apply here. For this reason, whenever I cast counters with fiber-optic lights, I always require complete artistic license from my clients. I advise them in advance to expect some areas of the counter to be brighter and others to be more subtle. Some glass chunks will catch the light during the day, others will only show off their sparkle at night. Clients who appreciate original art will be thrilled with the distinctive nature of their finished piece. But if a homeowner is not comfortable with the concept of artistic license, don't attempt to create a one-of-kind counter like this for them.

You've done it! You've designed a beautiful, functional outdoor kitchen that will bring your family and friends together to enjoy the pleasure of cooking and dining al fresco. I hope the information in this book helps you enjoy your outdoor kitchen as much as I enjoy designing them, and that your new space will help you celebrate life, savor good food, and create wonderful memories together. And remember, **"Every project is a self-portrait of the person who did the work. Autograph your work with excellence!" – Scott Cohen**

Layout Guides

Use this page as a design tool. Photocopy and cut out the appliances and layouts from the previous page to help determine how much space your outdoor kitchen will require.

1 Box = 1 square foot

Scale :1"= 4'

Layout Guides

Use this page as a design tool. Photocopy and cut out the appliances and layouts from the previous page to help determine how much space your outdoor kitchen will require.

1 Box = 1 square foot

Scale :1"= 4'

Template Sheet:

Photo copy and cut out to assist with your layout.

BBQ Accessories

Grill	Side Burner	Sink	Garnish Center	Beverage Center
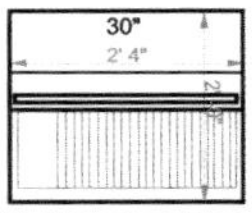 30" 2' 4"	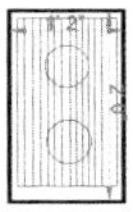	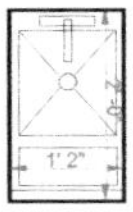 1' 2"	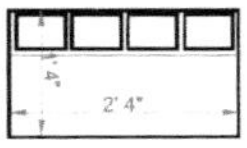 2' 4"	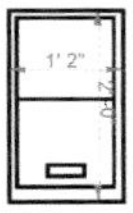 1' 2"
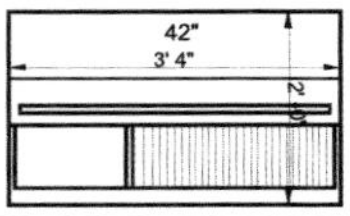 42" 3' 4"				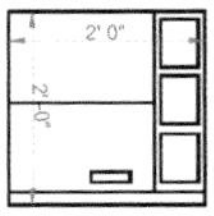 2' 0"
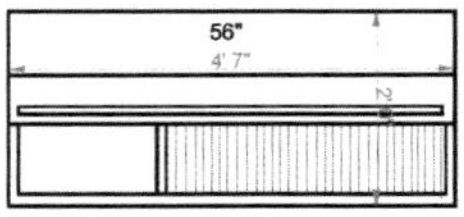 56" 4' 7"				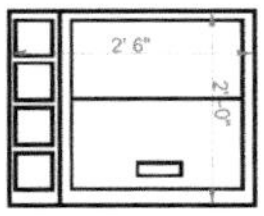 2' 6"

Tables

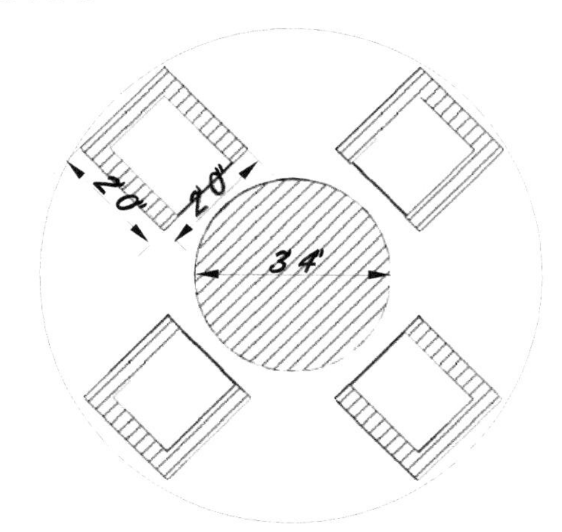

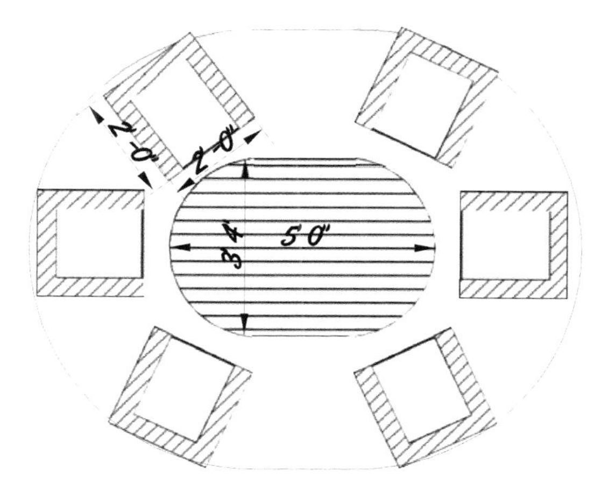

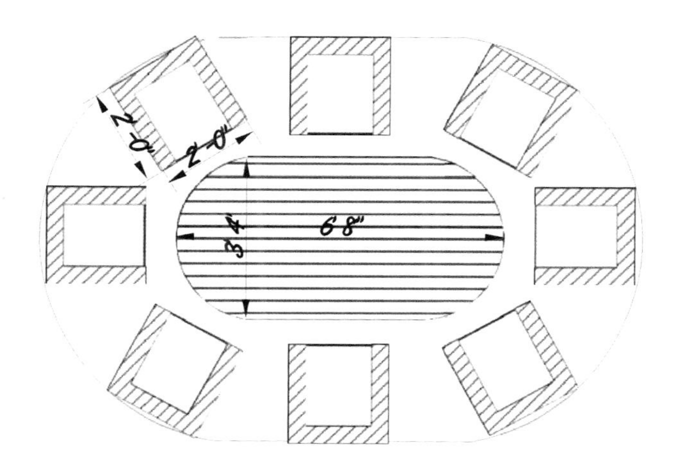

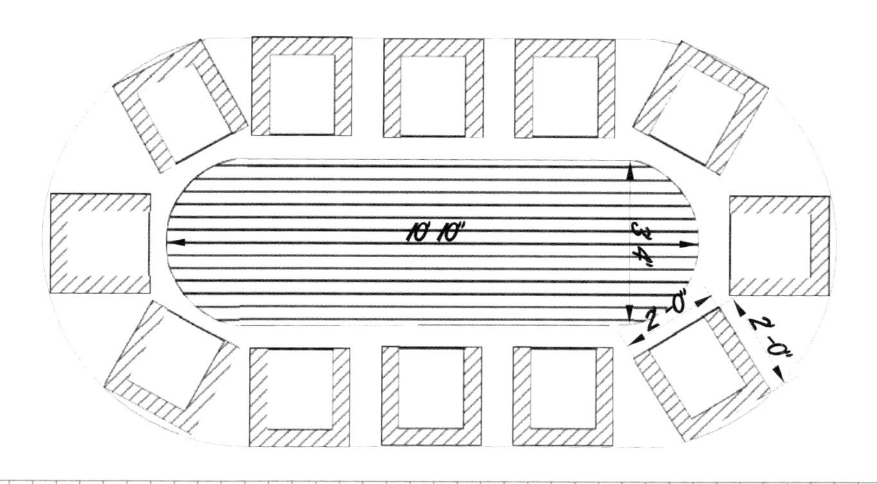

Wood Arbors

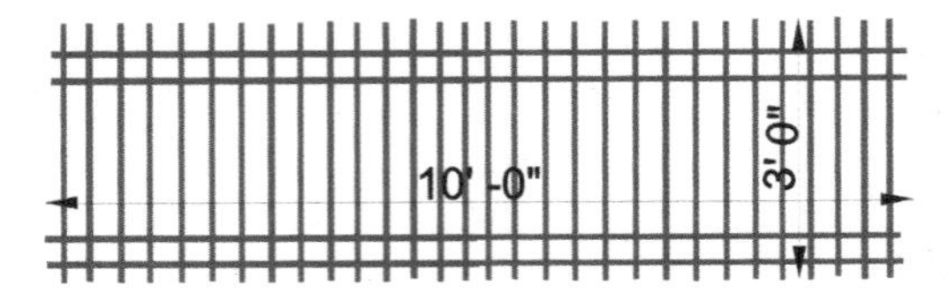

Gazebos

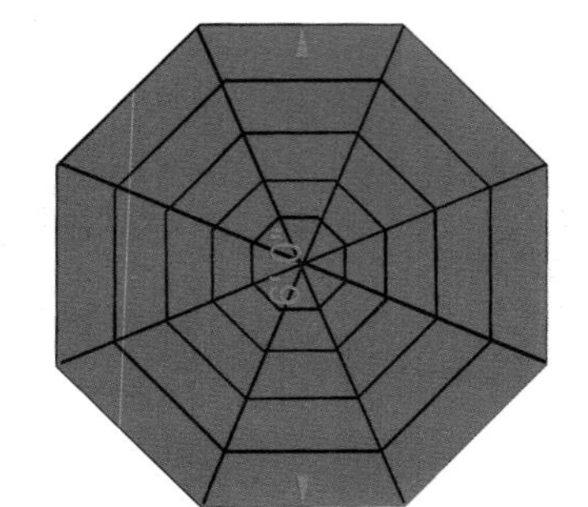

Iron Arbor

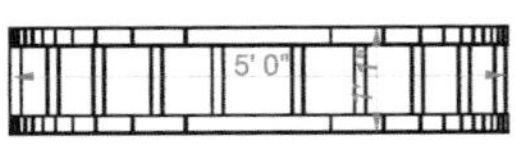

Bridges

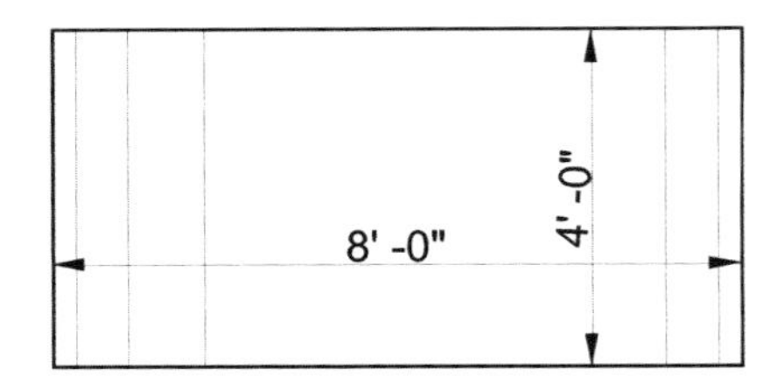

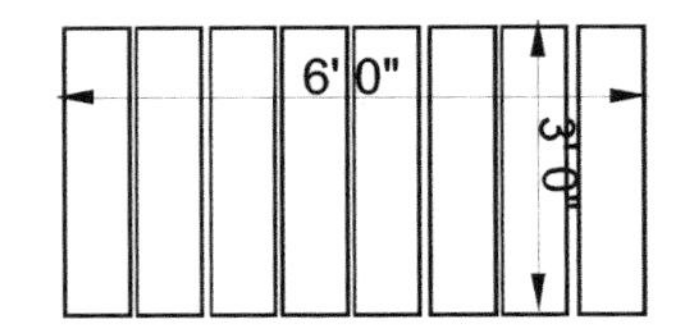

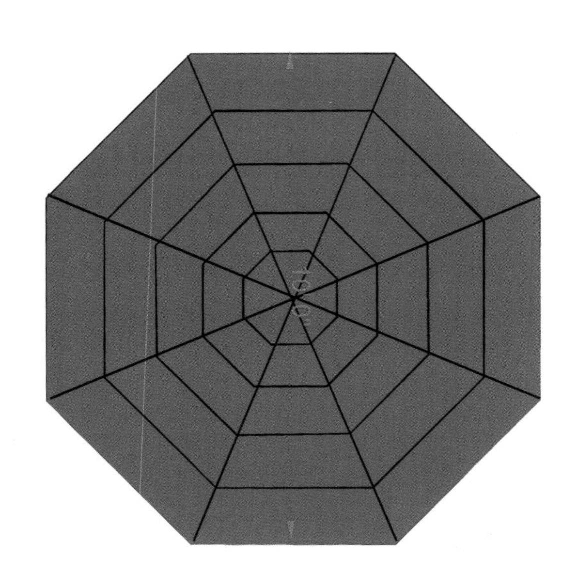

Umbrellas

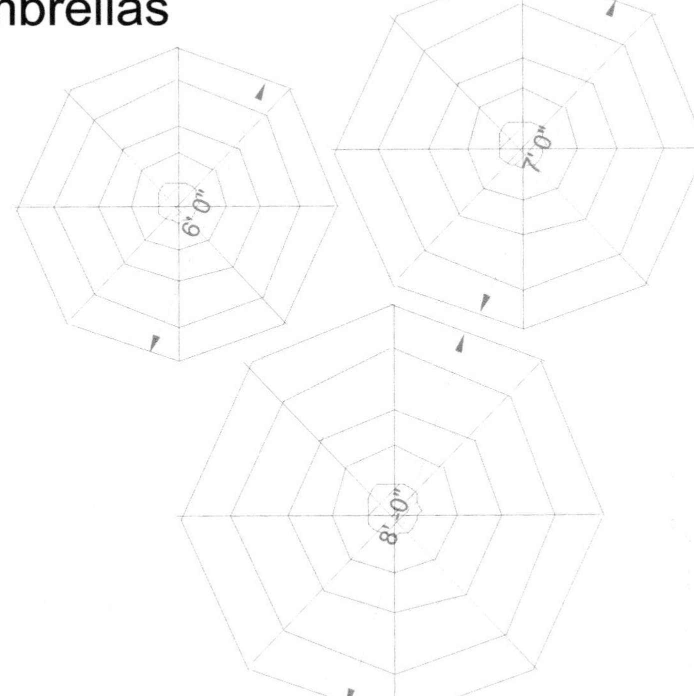

Sofa Sets

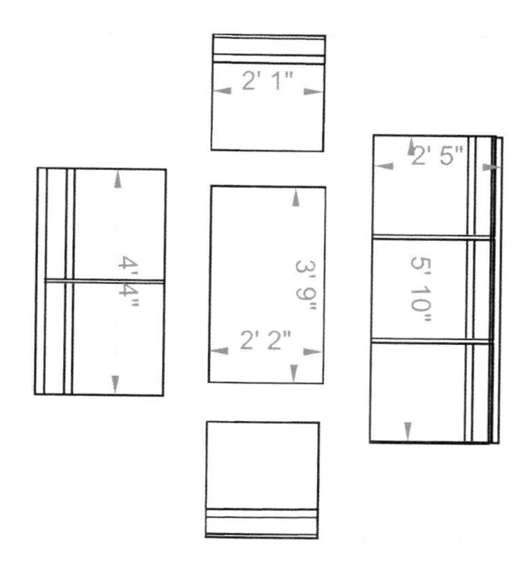

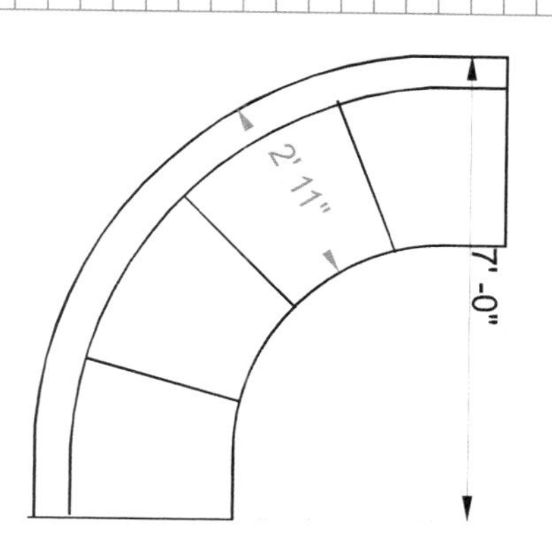

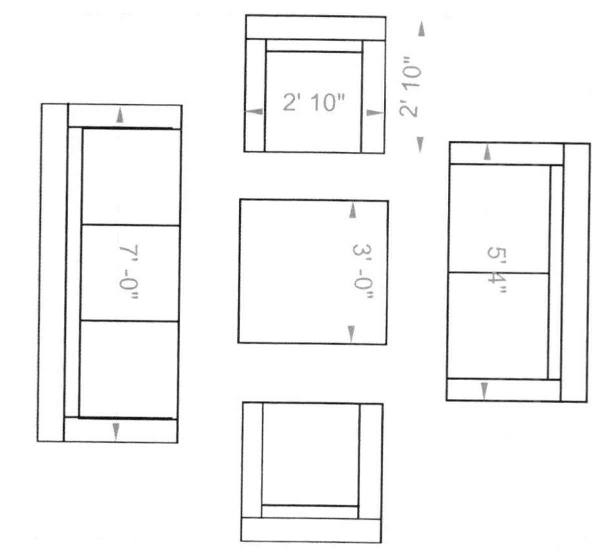

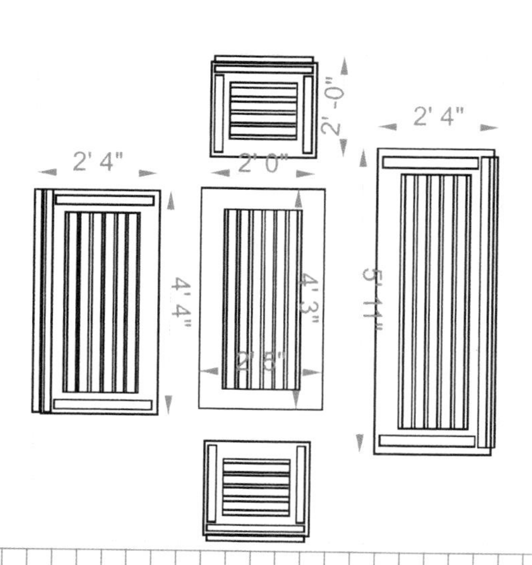

Tables

3' 10"
2' 2"

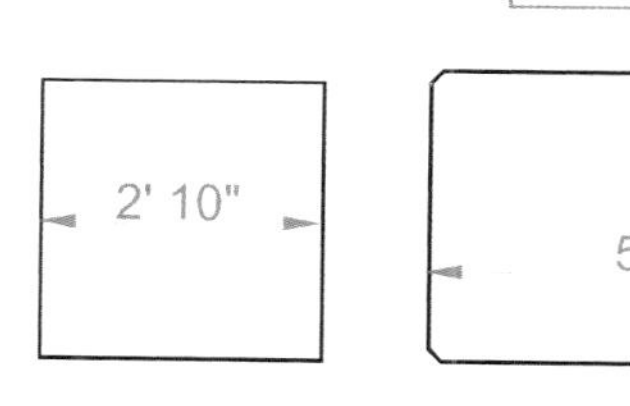

Coffee Tables

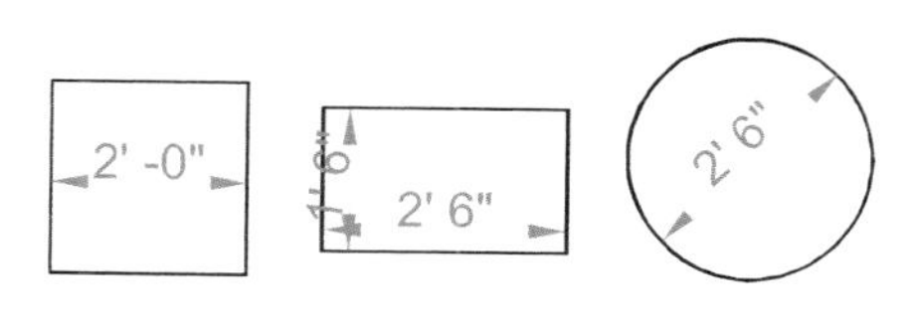

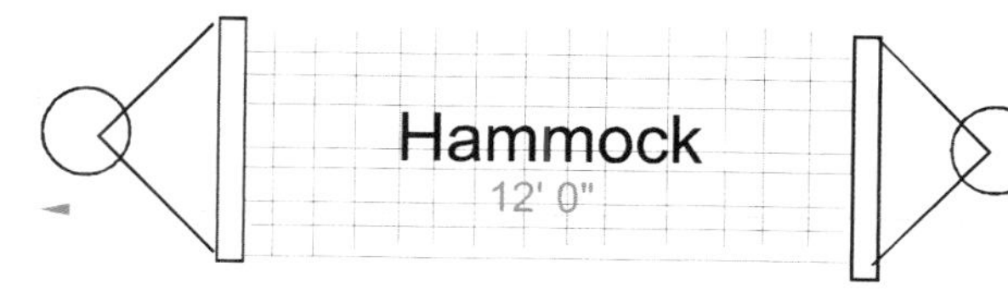

Garden Swing

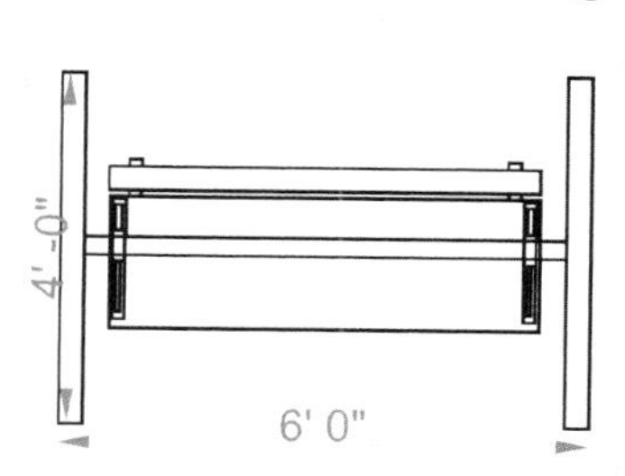

Spas

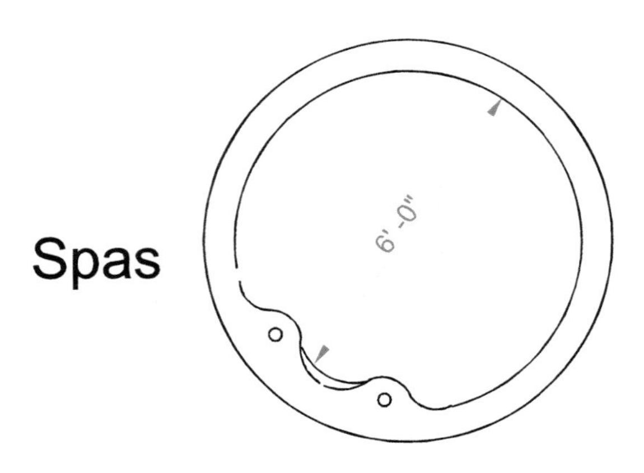

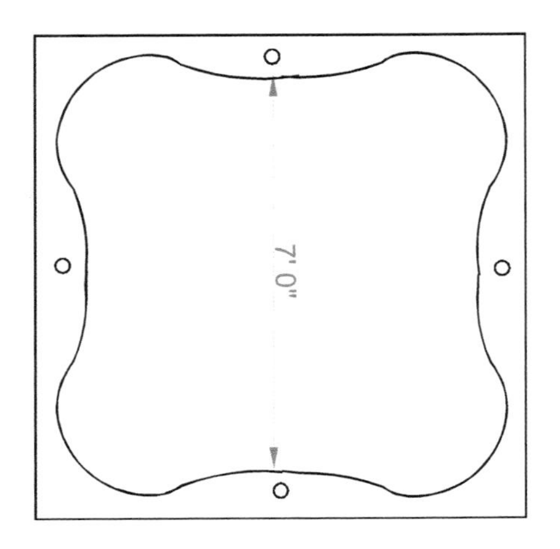

Fountains

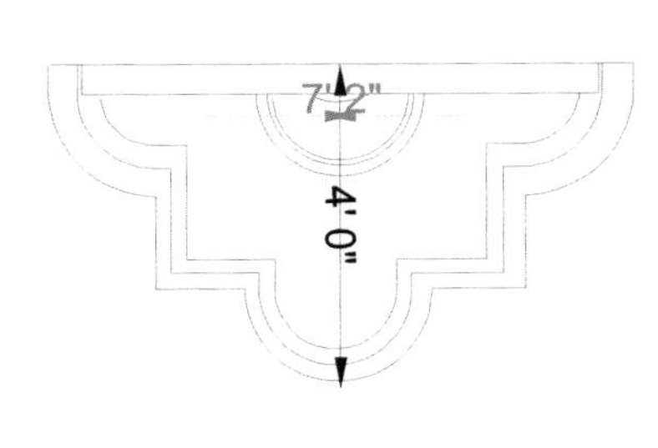

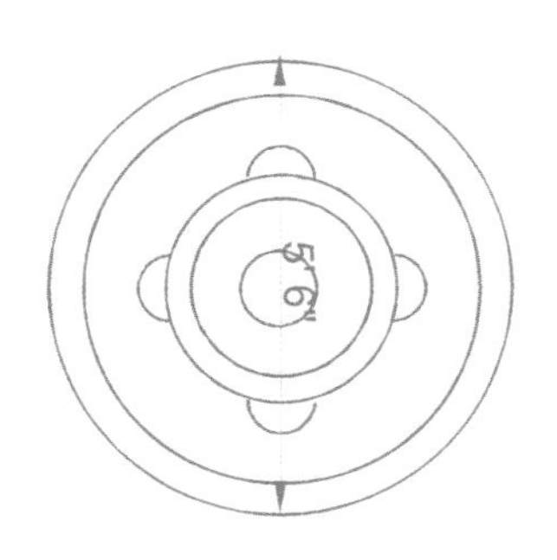

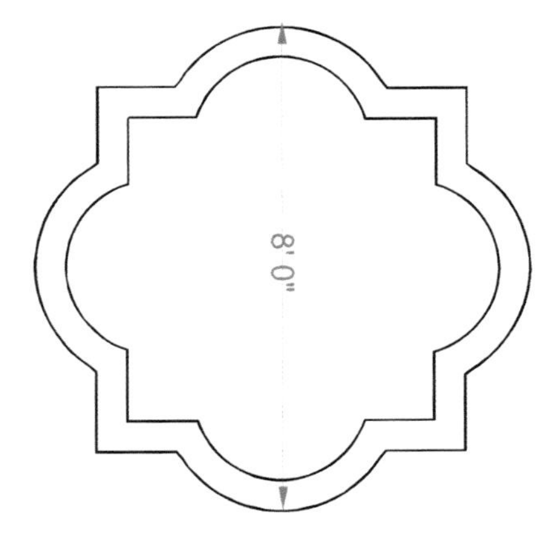

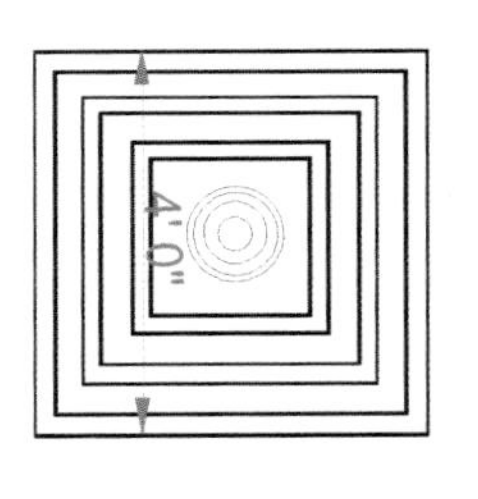

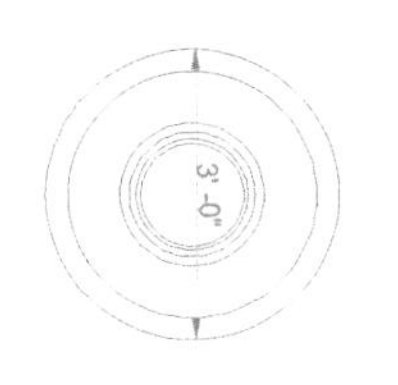

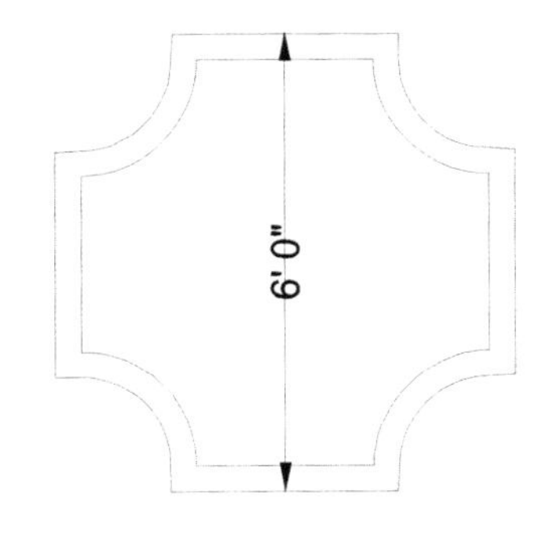

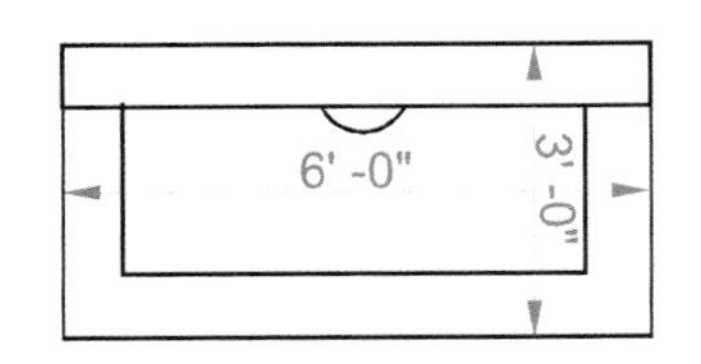

Benches

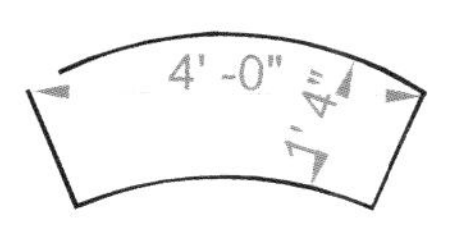

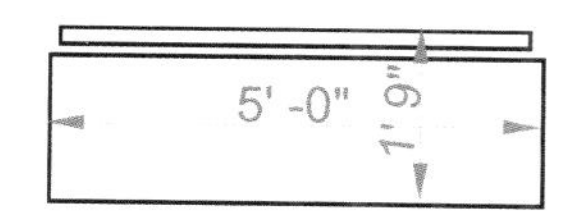

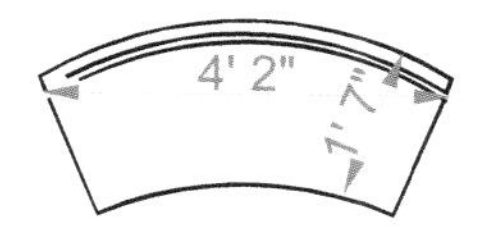

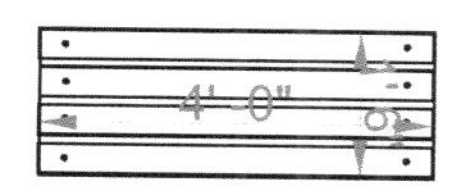

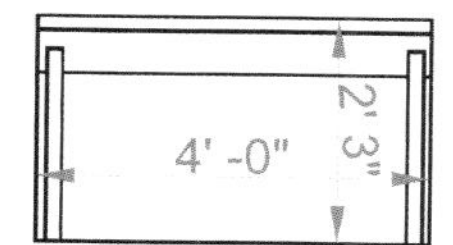

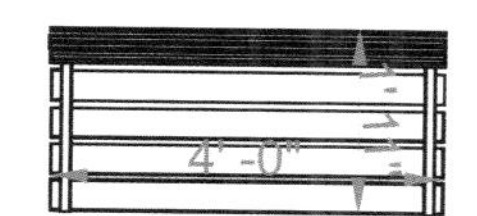

Stools

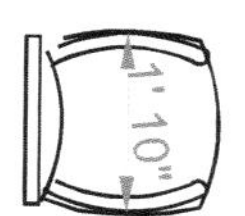

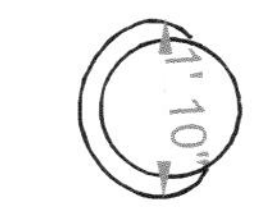

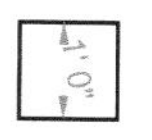

Chaise Lounges

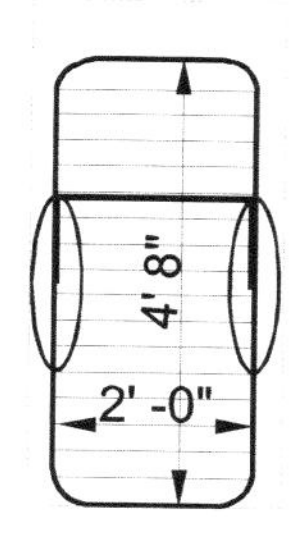

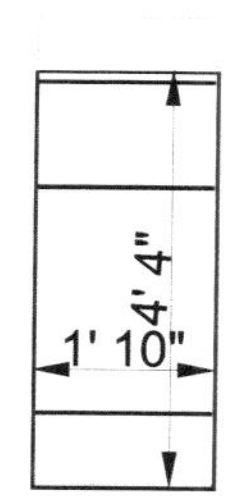

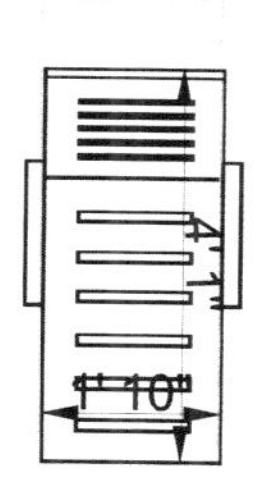

Dining Chairs

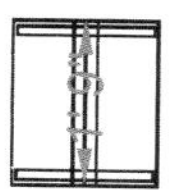

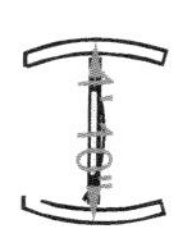

Chairs

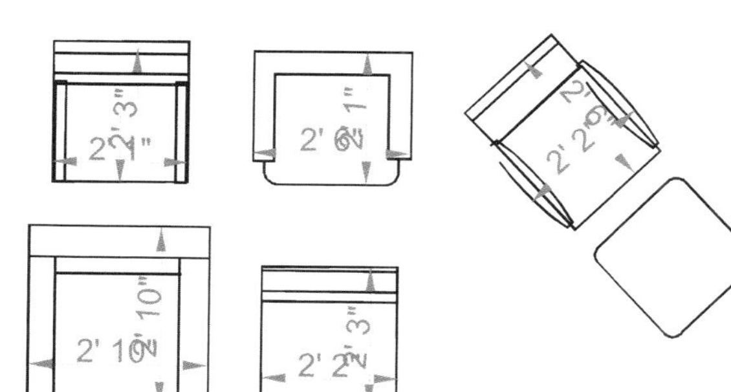

Adirondack Chair

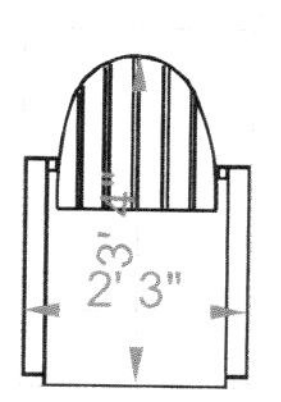

Rocking chair

2' 6"
2' -0"

Ottomans

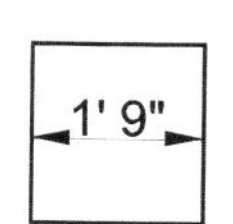

Double Ottoman

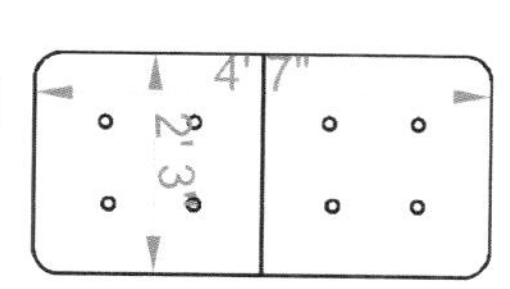

Fire Pits

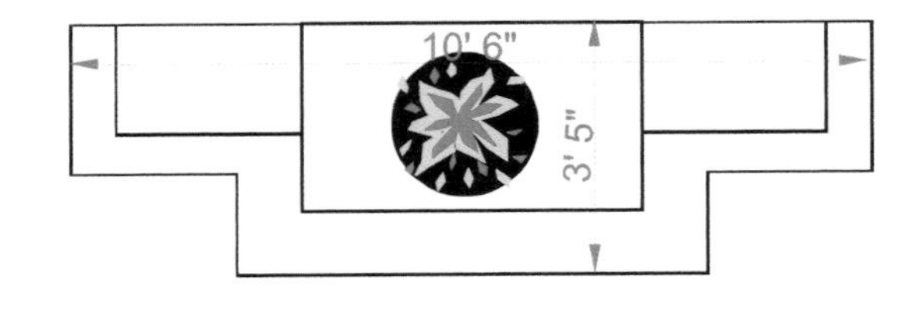

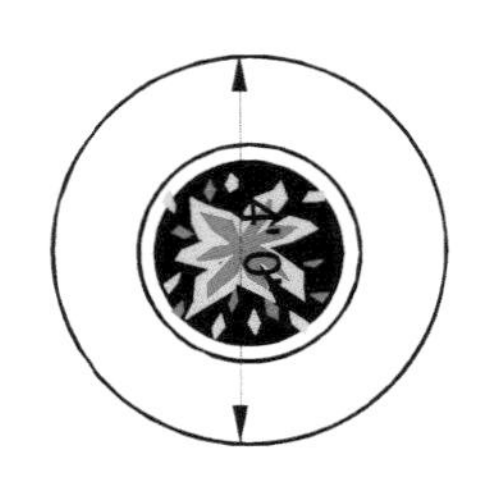

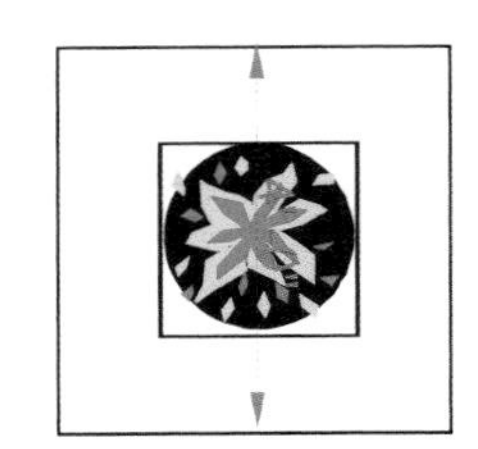

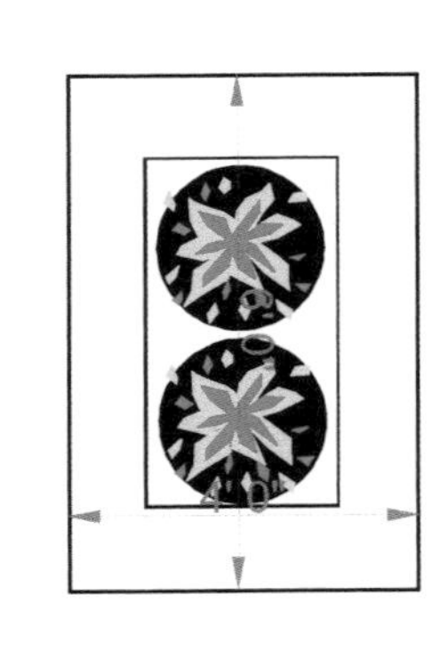

Pots

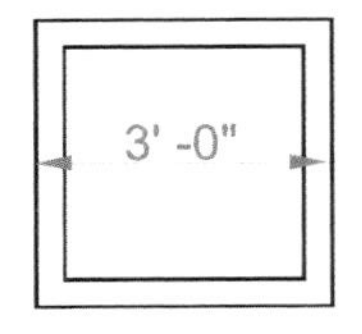

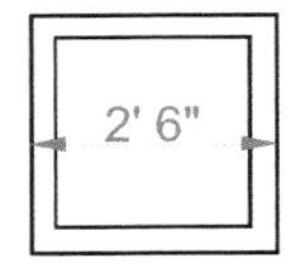

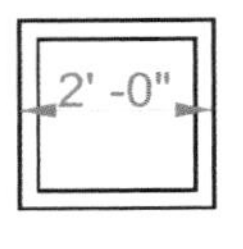

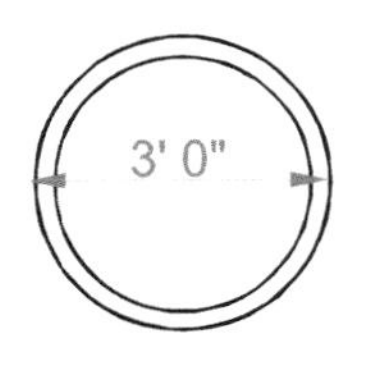

Bird Baths

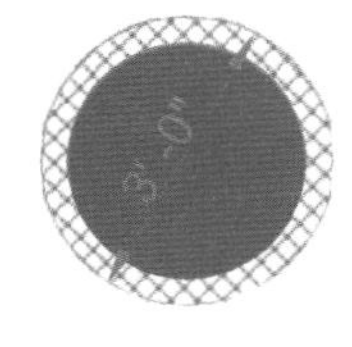

Scuppers

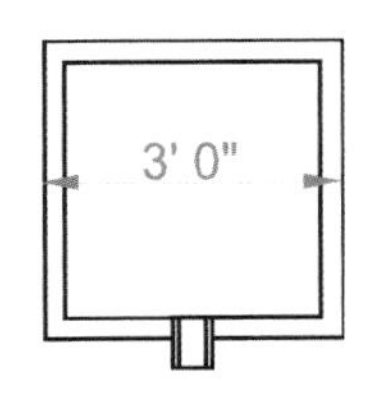

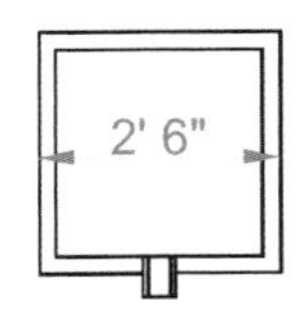

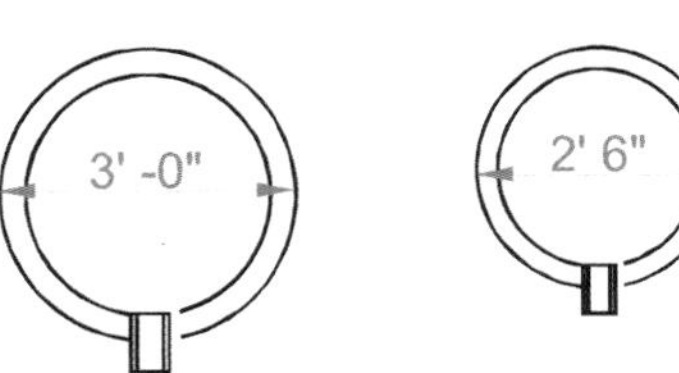

Pilasters

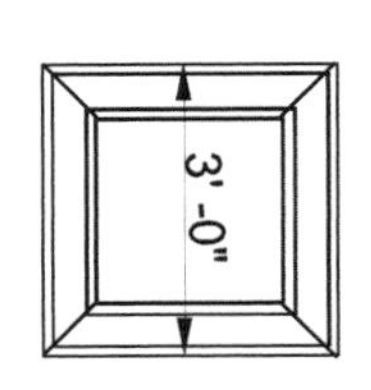

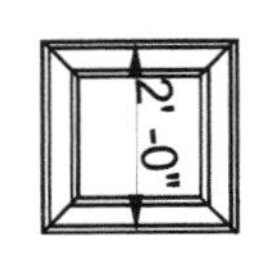

Pergolas

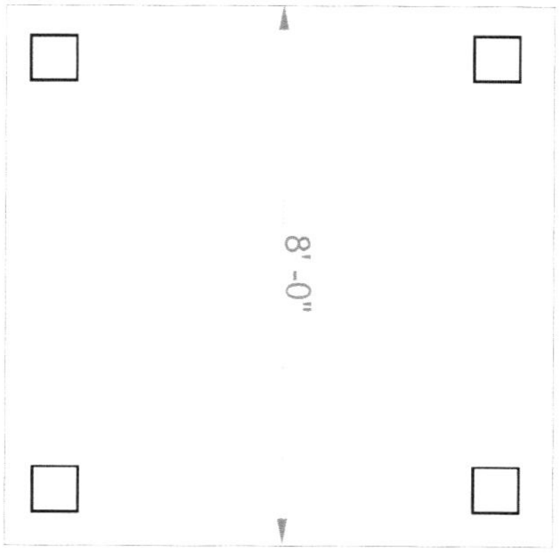

8' -0"

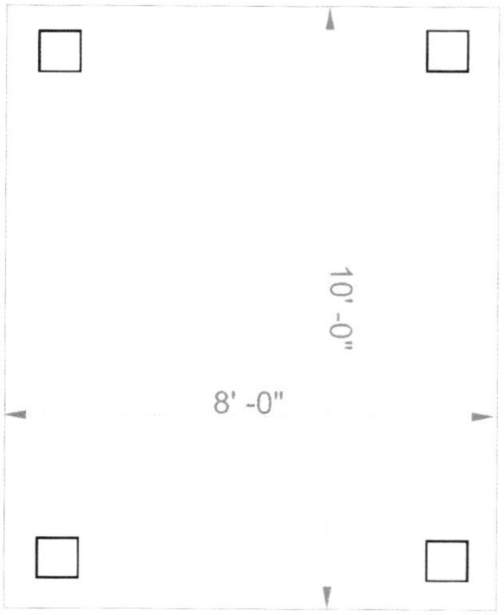

10' -0"

8' -0"

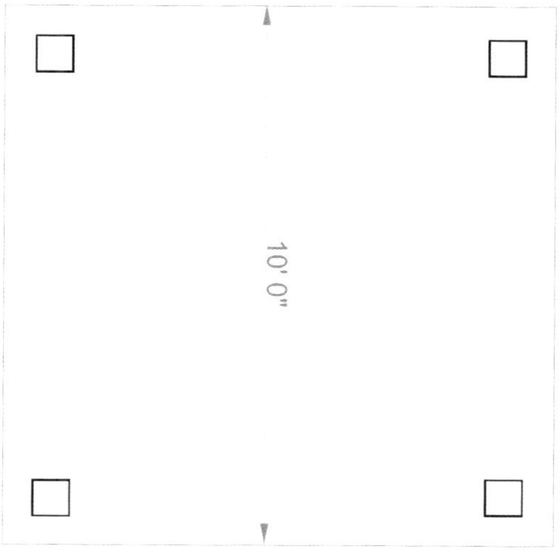

10' 0"

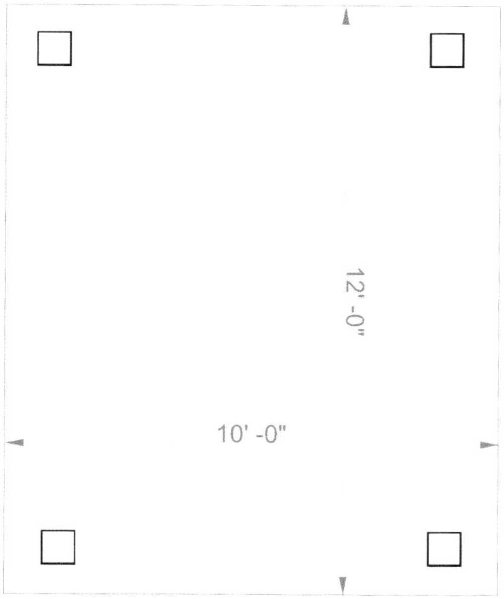

12' -0"

10' -0"

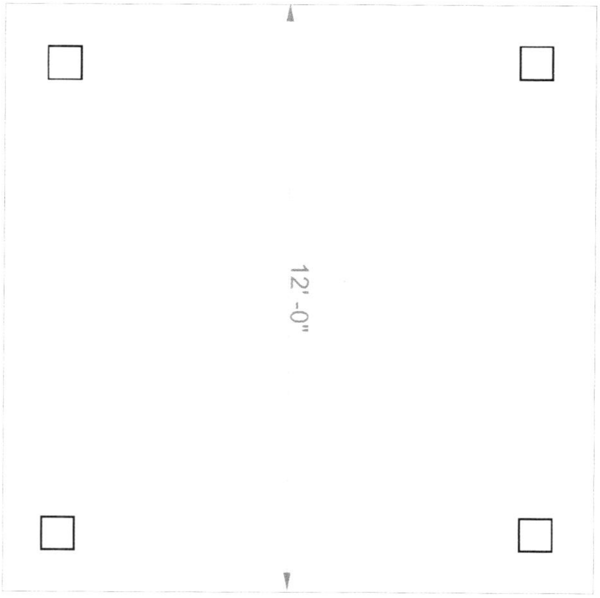

12' -0"

Photographers:

Nick Lucero
Deidra Walpole
Paul C. Jonason
Scott Cohen
Patrick Stringer
Jose Hernandez

Resources and Contributors:

ScottCohenDesigns.com
The Green Scene
6810 Canoga Ave., Canoga Park, CA. 91303
(818) 227-0740
GreenSceneLandscape.com
Fetch-A-Sketch.com
OutdoorKitchenDesignIdeas.com

AlfrescoGrills.com
AmericanSpecialtyGlass.com
Calgacrete.com
ConcreteNetwork.com
HarmonyOutdoorLiving.com
KalamazooGourmet.com
SpacePlanning.com
VerdantCustomOutdoors.com

About the Authors

Scott Cohen in his creative workspace

Scott Cohen is a nationally acclaimed garden artisan whose award winning work is frequently featured on Home and Garden Television and in numerous national books and magazines. He's known for his unique use of recycled materials, expert detailing, and innovative ceramic techniques to create stunning and functional outdoor environments.

Cohen is president and supervising designer of The Green Scene, a premier outdoor design and construction firm based in Canoga Park, California. He provides consultation for clients nationwide and gives seminars on designing outdoor kitchens and rooms, cast concrete techniques, and other topics for swimming pool and landscape professionals.

Elizabeth Lexau is a writer who frequently covers landscaping, garden design, and other outdoor living topics. She lives with her husband and two daughters near the shores of Lake Superior in Northern Wisconsin.

Made in the USA
Lexington, KY
21 April 2011

GREYSCALE

BIN TRAVELER FORM

Cut By William W Qty 53 Date 04-25-25

Scanned By__________ Qty__________ Date__________

Scanned Batch IDs

Notes / Exception